Caribbean Social Studies 4

St Lucia

Andrew Roberts

MACMILLAN
CARIBBEAN

Macmillan Education
Between Towns Road, Oxford OX4 3PP
A division of Macmillan Publishers Limited
Companies and representatives throughout the world

www.macmillan-caribbean.com

ISBN 0 333 95943 4

First published 1993, this edition 2003

Illustrated by Felicity Cary, Edna Moore and TechType

Authors' acknowledgements

The author and publishers wish to acknowledge, with thanks, the following
photographic sources.
Associated Press pp 99; 106
Anne Bolt pp 9; 11; 59; 73 left; 82
Micheal Bourne pp 17; 21; 23 top; 35; 57 centre and below; 58; 66; 92; 97
above and below
COMPIX p 41 left
Robert Harding Picture Library p 67 right
Chris Huxley p 23 centre
Bill Lennox pp 1; 10; 13; 14; 31; 57 above; 63; 65 all photographs;
67 left; 73 right; 86 below; 96; 101
Life File p 49 (Paul Richards)
Picturepoint pp 7; 60 (NASA)
Andrew Roberts pp 5; 8; 20; 23 below; 51; 56; 98
Spectrum Picture Library p 42
Cecile Wiltshire pp 16; 86 above; 95
The cover photograph is courtesy of Chris Huxley

The publishers have made every effort to trace the copyright holders but if
they heve inadvertently overlooked any, they will be pleased to make the
necessary arrangements at the first opportunity.

Printed and bound in Malaysia

2007 2006 2005 2004 2003
10 9 8   7 6 5 4 3 2 1

Contents

The landscape

Imagine that you are flying in a helicopter over our country. What are the things which you might see? You might see hills, rivers, forests, the sea, fields, beaches, cliffs, towns, villages, factories and roads.

This photograph was taken from a helicopter. What can you see in this landscape?

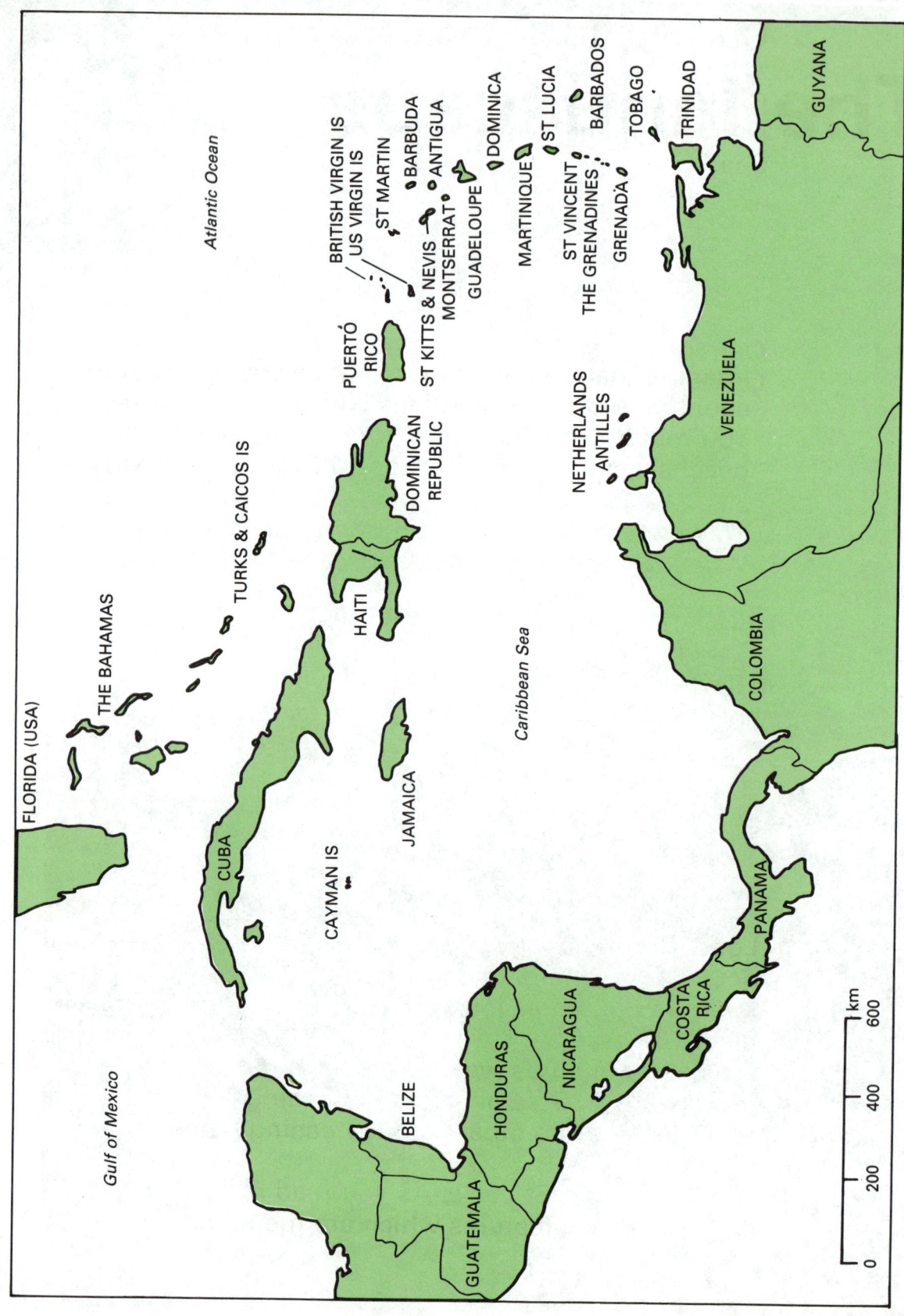

Atlantic Ocean

FLORIDA (USA)

THE BAHAMAS

TURKS & CAICOS IS

Gulf of Mexico

CUBA

CAYMAN IS

JAMAICA

HAITI

DOMINICAN REPUBLIC

PUERTO RICO

BRITISH VIRGIN IS
US VIRGIN IS
ST MARTIN
BARBUDA
ANTIGUA
ST KITTS & NEVIS
MONTSERRAT
GUADELOUPE
DOMINICA
MARTINIQUE
ST LUCIA
BARBADOS
TOBAGO
ST VINCENT
THE GRENADINES
GRENADA
TRINIDAD

NETHERLANDS ANTILLES

Caribbean Sea

BELIZE

GUATEMALA

HONDURAS

NICARAGUA

COSTA RICA

PANAMA

COLOMBIA

VENEZUELA

GUYANA

km
0   200   400   600

2

Our country in the Caribbean

Our country is part of the Caribbean Region. The countries in this region are all near the Caribbean Sea.

Find the Caribbean Sea on the map. Write down the names of the countries bordering the Caribbean Sea. How many have you written down?

Our country is called **St Lucia**. It is in the east of the Caribbean Region.

Find Antigua, St Vincent, Guadeloupe and Barbados. In which direction are they from our country?

The natural landscape

Think of all the different features you saw from the helicopter. We call these *physical features*. Some of the features are natural. Others are made by people.

In the next few pages, we shall look at some of the natural features which you might see.

1 Look up *physical features* in the *glossary* and write down its meaning. Every time you see words in *italics* in this book, look them up in the glossary on page 107.
2 Divide the features we can see from our helicopter into two lists. Give one list the heading **Natural features**, and the other list the heading **Man-made features**.
3 Draw a map of St Lucia. As you read the next few pages, add the features which are mentioned to your map.

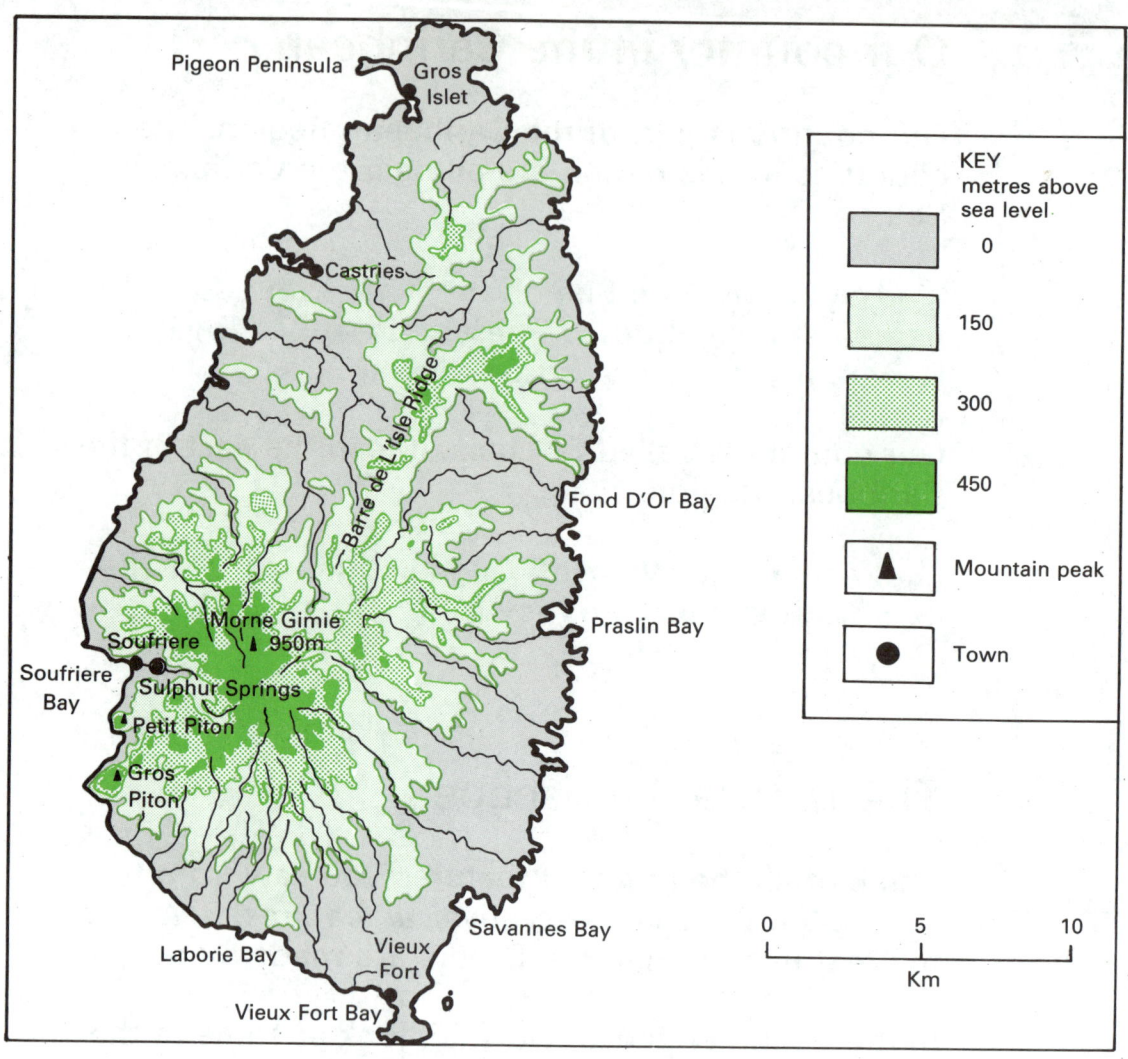

Map Key:

KEY
metres above sea level
- 0
- 150
- 300
- 450
- ▲ Mountain peak
- ● Town

Map labels: Pigeon Peninsula, Gros Islet, Castries, Barre de L'Isle Ridge, Fond D'Or Bay, Praslin Bay, Morne Gimie ▲ 950m, Soufriere, Soufriere Bay, Sulphur Springs, Petit Piton, Gros Piton, Savannes Bay, Vieux Fort, Laborie Bay, Vieux Fort Bay

Scale: 0 — 5 — 10 Km

Coastal strips

The land which is close to the sea is called the *coastal strip*. On the map it is shown by a light shading. Another name for the coastal strip is the **coastal plain**. The coastal strip lies between the sea and the hills and mountains in the centre of our country. In some places there are beaches. The coastal plain is much wider in some places than in others. For example, in the south-east of St Lucia, between Praslin Bay and Vieux Fort Bay, the coastal strip is quite wide. In the north of the country near Gros Islet we can find a wide coastal strip. In some places the coastal strip is narrow. The hills and mountains rise steeply from the coastline.

Around the coastline there are many *bays*. A bay is a place where the land surrounds the sea on three sides. Bays often give shelter from strong winds to ships and boats.

Roseau Bay

Look at the physical map of St Lucia opposite. Find the areas where the coastal strip is wide and areas which have very little or no coastal strip.

Cliffs

In many places along the western coast of St Lucia and also in some places along the eastern coast, there is very little coastal strip. In these areas the rocks and mountains rise steeply from the sea. These areas where the land rises or drops sharply are called cliffs. But it is not only near the sea that one can find cliffs. In fact wherever land drops steeply to lower land the area can be called a cliff. One can therefore find many cliffs in the mountains in the centre of the

5

island. Those of you who travel to Castries from the eastern and southern parts of the country will be able to see many cliffs as you travel along the Barre de L'Isle road. The next time you travel either along the highways or to the garden with your parents, look for areas which are cliffs.

Look at the picture of a cliff above. Do you know any area where the land drops like this?

Rivers

In St Lucia there are several rivers. They all begin in the mountains in the interior of the island. This area is called the watershed. All the rivers begin as small watercourses or ravines but as they flow towards the coast they join with others at different places. Eventually they become much larger and are called rivers.

Look at your atlas and name two rivers that flow into the sea on the western coast of St Lucia, and two that flow into the sea on the eastern coast of the island.

Hills and mountains

In St Lucia there are many areas of highland. We measure their height against the level of the sea around the island, either in feet or metres. These areas of high land are given special names. When the highland areas are less than 1000 feet (310 metres) high they are called hills. Those which are more than 310 metres are called mountains. The biggest group of mountains in St Lucia is in the central part of the island. A group of mountains is called a *mountain range*. Among the mountains in the centre of the island, the tallest is called Morne Gimie. You can see Morne Gimie from Anse La Raye in the photograph below.

Not very far from Morne Gimie and just to the south of the town of Soufriere are two of the most beautiful natural features of our country. These are the Pitons: Gros Piton (796 m or 2619 ft) and Petit Piton (750 m

or 2461 ft). You can see Petit Piton in the photograph.

Why were the Pitons given that special name?

■ ■ Study the map of St Lucia on page 4 carefully. Use the map, your atlas and what you have learned on pages 1 to 8 to answer these questions.

1 Name five mountain peaks above 500 metres above sea level.
2 Which is the highest mountain peak in St Lucia?
3 When does a hill become a mountain?
4 In which part of St Lucia is the coastal strip widest?
5 In which part of St Lucia is the highest land?
6 Where is the St Lucia channel?
7 From which piece of land does this channel divide St Lucia?
8 Which very large area of water surrounds St Lucia?
9 Name five bays around the coast of St Lucia.
10 Work out which are the three longest rivers in St Lucia, using the scale line on the map.

The Sulphur Springs

Also near the town of Soufriere are the Sulphur Springs. See them in the photograph. They are very famous, and give Soufriere its name.

What does Soufriere mean?

These springs are part of a volcano which has not erupted for many thousands of years. However, this volcano is not *extinct.* Its crater contains bubbling springs which give off hot gases. This is called a **solfatara**.

Find the Sulphur Springs on the map of St Lucia on page 4.

The Sulphur Springs have been an important resource for St Lucia in several ways:
1 In the 18th century, the French king Louis XVI built baths at the Sulphur Springs so that his soldiers could benefit from bathing in the sulphurous water from the Springs. These baths were believed to heal and refresh those who used them.

*The Diamond
Mineral Baths
at Soufriere*

2 A hundred years ago, sulphur from the Springs
was an important export.

3 It is possible that the Springs may be useful in the
future as a source of **geothermal energy**. This is a
type of energy which uses the enormous heat of
the inner part of the Earth. This might be very
helpful to our economy, but it would be expensive
to extract.

4 The Springs are an important tourist attraction.
Many tourists visit them each year.

1 List the ways in which the Sulphur Springs are
important to St Lucia. Start with the **most
important** way. Explain why you have listed
them in this order.

2 Write down the meaning of these words and
phrases: *extinct   solfatara   geothermal energy*

3 Find out more about the element called **sulphur**.
What are its chemical properties? How might
sulphurous water be healing and refreshing if you
bathe in it? Your teacher will help you.

Mangrove forests

Look at the picture above. If you walk or fly along the south-eastern coast of St Lucia you will see fairly large trees growing in the shallow sea water. Most other trees would not be able to grow in this kind of *environment*.

Many people think that these clumps of mangrove are just a group of useless trees. Others think that the only value in mangrove forests is to have them cut to make charcoal. Mangrove forests are in fact very useful to us. If you go among the mangrove and examine it carefully you will find the area very interesting. Many large fish go among the mangrove to lay their eggs and the young fish remain there until they are able to go into the open sea on their own. The leaves of the mangrove fall into the water and as they rot they become a source of food for small fish.

Mangrove forests not only protect small fish and provide them with food. They serve as homes for many species of birds. It is common to see many birds' nests among the branches. The mangrove trees also help to protect the coast from erosion during storms and hurricanes. The large numbers of roots and thick stems break the force of the waves preventing them from lashing with great force on to the shore.

Unfortunately, mangrove forests are in danger of complete destruction. This is so because people cut them down to make charcoal much faster then they can grow back again. The government is trying to encourage people to use other trees for making charcoal. Mangrove forests are too important to lose.

CLASS DISCUSSION
Discuss these questions in a group or in class with your teacher.
a) Why should we save the mangrove forest?
b) What can we do to protect our mangrove forest?

The man-made landscape

Some of our landscape has been made by people. We call this the man-made landscape.

Towns
Towns have many buildings made by people. They are therefore part of the man-made landscape. In our country there are some important towns. Let us look at two of them.

Castries
In many countries, the largest towns are called *cities*. The largest town in our country is Castries. It is a city. Castries is also the **capital city** of our country.

Make a special study of Castries city. Below and on pages 14 and 15 there are photographs, diagrams and a history of Castries to help you. Study these carefully. Use them for the following activities:

1 Write down the names of the suburban communities where people who work in Castries live.
2 Describe the appearance of the city. Use some of these words: beautiful, large, trees, ancient, modern, buildings, river, sea.
3 Use Table 1 and the pie chart to answer these questions:
   a) What percentage of the whole population of St Lucia lives in Castries?
   b) Compare the population of Castries with that of Vieux Fort. Explain why the population of Castries is so much bigger.
4 Find out more about the public buildings of Castries.
5 Write two paragraphs about the history of Castries between 1763 and 1990.

Table 1 Population

Town or country	Population (1990)
St Lucia	141 300
Castries	55 022
Vieux Fort	12 951

The first settlement in the Castries area was not where the city is now. The first settlement was near the Vigie Marina. This settlement was called La Carenage. Around 1763 the town was moved to its present site. The new name, Castries, was given to the town. Castries was named after a French Minister, Charles de Castries.

The town suffered many problems such as hurricanes, earthquakes, floods and fires. The fires destroyed many buildings. In 1927 the main business area of Castries was destroyed by fire. In 1948 more than three-quarters of the town was destroyed by a fire which started in a tailor's shop. Over 2000 people became homeless because of that fire.

Castries grew rapidly. Many people from the villages and towns went to live in Castries. As the population increased, people moved into *suburban* areas such as Ceders, Entrepot, Sans Souci and the Morne. As time went on, many new stores and offices were built in the city. More schools were built for the increasing population. In 1960 for example, there were only two secondary schools in the entire district. In 1991, there were six secondary schools in the city of Castries.

Today even the suburban parts of Castries such as Entrepot and the Morne are becoming overcrowded. As soon as the highway between Castries and Gros Islet was completed large numbers of people started building their homes all along the road. Castries is quickly becoming joined to Gros Islet into one large housing and business area.

More and more people are leaving the city centre to live in the suburban areas. The land that they leave behind is being used to set up more business places. Although there are fewer people living in the city centre, the population of the Castries area as a whole is still increasing steadily. At the present time there are over 50 000 people living in the Castries area.

Castries is a very busy city with lots of stores and other business places. The seaport is always busy with either cargo or tourist ships.

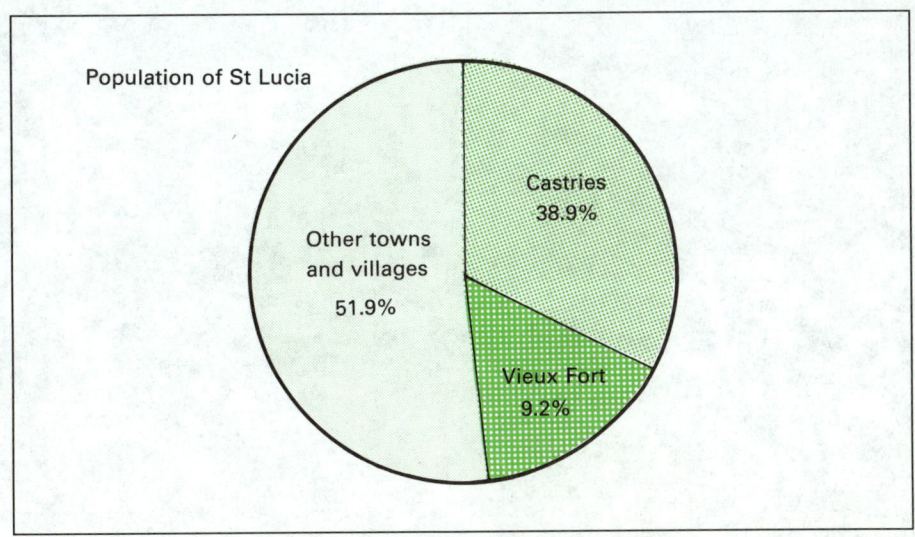

Population of St Lucia

Other towns and villages 51.9%

Castries 38.9%

Vieux Fort 9.2%

Vieux Fort

The second largest town in our country is called Vieux Fort. This town is in the southern part of our country. The coastal strip around the town of Vieux Fort is very wide.

Is the coastal strip around Castries wide or narrow?

Long ago a lot of sugar cane was grown in the area. You can still see the remains of an old sugar mill in an area close to the airport.

During the second world war, Vieux Fort was a very active town. Many people had moved to this town to work on the military base which was being built by the Americans. This old military base was later converted into our country's main airport, Hewanorra.

One of the most interesting sites in the Vieux Fort area is the Moule-A-Chique Peninsula. If you go to the top of the hill at Moule-A-Chique, you will have a very beautiful view of Vieux Fort and a large part of the island.

Town of Vieux Fort taken from Moule-A-Chique

As the number of industries in Vieux Fort increase, the population of the town keeps growing steadily. There are several factories which produce various items of clothing, household and building materials. Also, two of the most important factories in our country are in Vieux Fort. They are the Winera box-making factory and the Heineken Brewery. Winera produces boxes in which our country's bananas are shipped to Europe. The Heineken Brewery produces beer and malt for sale locally as well as for export to other Caribbean countries.

Many people in Vieux Fort work in stores, offices, factories and hotels but there are also many people who make a living from fishing. Although Vieux Fort is becoming more and more an *industrial* town, fishing remains an important way of earning a living.

Castries and Vieux Fort are *urban* settlements. This makes them different from *rural* settlements like the villages of our country. In the photo you can see another urban settlement.

The village of
Canaries on
the West coast

GROUP WORK

1 Discuss with the rest of your group what makes an urban settlement different from a rural one.
2 Make a group list of things which would happen often in an urban settlement but not in a rural one.

The way we live

My name is Chris. I live in a small village on the west coast. The name of my village is Canaries. My family owns a fishing boat. My father earns his living by fishing. I like to help him in the boat.

On weekdays and sometimes on Saturdays, my father and three of his friends go out to sea. As the boats come in from the sea many villagers come down to the shore to buy fish. Sometimes the catch is small, but sometimes they catch a lot of fish. I like to help my father when he makes fish pots or mends his fishing nets. One day I would like to go out to sea with my father to see what it is like on the open ocean.

My name is Angella. I live in a village not close to the coast. It is called Saltibus. My family grows bananas and vegetables such as carrots, cabbages, yams and dasheen. We sell the bananas to the Banana Association every fortnight. I like to go to the Boxing Plant to collect empty boxes with my father, and pack them in the shed in the garden to be used on the next banana day. We take the vegetables to the market in the town every Saturday. It is 16 kilometres to the nearest town from our home, and eight kilometres to

the sea. Sometimes on Saturdays I travel to town with my mother when she goes to sell at the market. I like to collect the money from the people who buy and give them their change.

My name is Saria. I live in the city of Castries. This part of Castries is called La Clery. My home is not far from Vigie Airport. From my home I can see the aircraft as they land and take off from the runway.

My home is also near the beach. Sometimes I go with my brother when he goes jogging along the beach in the mornings. My father works in a factory and my mother is a secretary in an office. We do not grow our own food. We buy either at the vegetable market or at one of the supermarkets in the city. Sometimes we are able to buy fresh fish from the fishermen as they return from their fishing trip, but most of the time we buy our fish from the Fishing Complex. I cannot help my parents in their work, but I help them to take care of the house.

These children live very different lives. Your way of life may be like the way of life of one of them. Perhaps it is different from all of them.

- **1** Write down the differences in the way they live. Give some reasons why they live different lives.
- **2** Write a few sentences about your family's way of life. Say where you live and how that affects what you and your family do.

How the landscape changes

The natural landscape does not stay the same all the time. Sometimes a hurricane or a landslide or an earthquake changes the landscape. Everything looks suddenly different. Sometimes changes come more slowly. People can change the landscape too.

Hurricanes

A hurricane is the strongest wind we have. We measure wind speed in kilometres per hour (kph) or miles per hour (mph). A hurricane blows at more than 120 kp/h (75 mph). Some gusts are more than 160 kp/h (100 mph). Hurricanes form in the Atlantic ocean east of the Caribbean Islands and move slowly westward. They come most often between June and October. Hurricanes can cause a great deal of damage. Just before a season begins, the *meteorologists* agree on a list of names by which hurricanes for the year will be called.

Which hurricanes can you remember? What damage did they do?

In the picture, you can see the damage done by Hurricane Allen in our country in August 1980. This hurricane caused a lot of damage to buildings. The roofs of many houses were blown away. Almost all the banana trees on the island were either blown down or washed away by flooded rivers. Many large trees were destroyed in the forest, and landslides damaged many roads. This made it impossible for people to travel to other places, except on foot, for many days.

Other natural changes

Rivers can cause great changes in the natural landscape of the country. When it rains heavily or for a long time, the rivers become flooded. As these rivers flow towards the sea, they *erode* their banks and take the soil to the sea. Sometimes they wash away so much soil in one area that only the bare rocks remain.

Soil erosion in Western St Lucia

Another natural *disaster* which took place in our country was the major landslide which occurred at Ravine Poisson near the Barre-de-L'Isle Ridge. It had rained for many days and the ground could not hold any more water. Some workmen were cleaning the road when suddenly, without any warning, the entire side of a hill slid down across the road and into the river, burying trees, houses and all the people in its path.

Many other landslides have occurred in St Lucia since the one at Ravine Poisson. People have not been killed but many acres of fertile land have been lost as a result of these landslides.

Man-made changes

People make changes to the natural landscape too. They divert rivers, reclaim land, cut down trees, build roads and do many other things. They also spoil the landscape by destroying and *polluting* the beautiful country we have.

Do people spoil your part of the country? How do they spoil it? What can be done to put this right?

Man can change the natural landscape very quickly by building houses in an area. In many parts of the country, areas which were covered with bush or large trees have been cleared to build homes, hotels and other buildings, making the area completely different. Some of the biggest changes are taking place in the Gros Islet area where a place which was once a swamp has been changed into a marina for yachts and land for hotels, restaurants and other business. In the surrounding areas, such as Cap and Mongiraud, large areas of bush have been cleared for housing.

Reclaiming the land

The coast near Rodney Bay was changed completely when the sea was *reclaimed*, joining the land to

The peninsula at Pigeon Island

Urban development in Castries – Pointe Seraphine shopping centre

The port at Vieux Fort, built on reclaimed land

Pigeon Island and forming a man-made *peninsula*. Land has also been reclaimed in many parts of the Castries harbour for port improvement. Point Seraphine shopping centre and part of the Vigie airport runway have been built on land reclaimed from the sea. Land is being reclaimed in order to improve the seaport at Vieux Fort.

Roads

We build roads so that we can travel from one part of our country to another. When land is cleared to build roads the landscape suddenly looks very different.

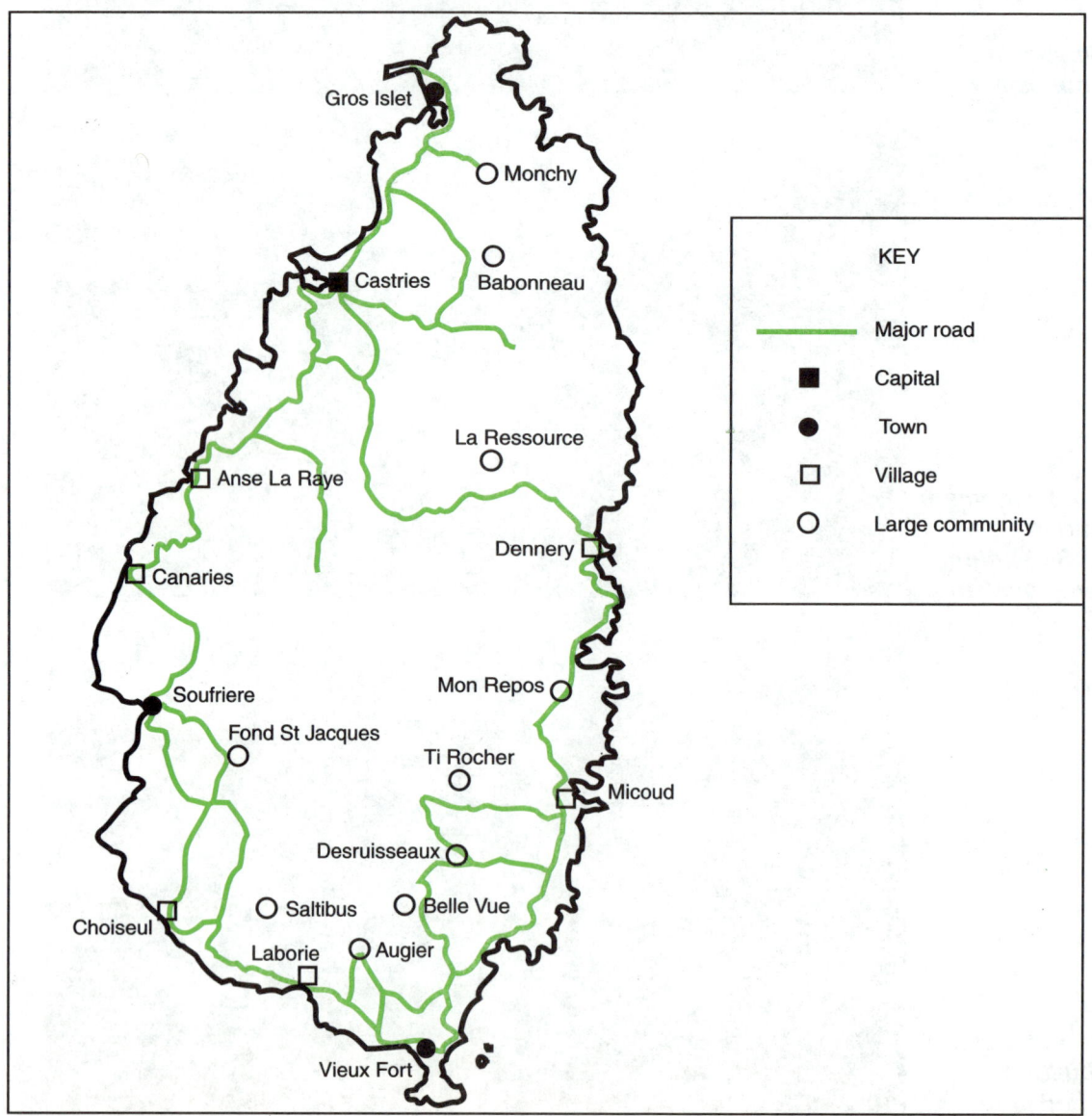

KEY

——	Major road
■	Capital
●	Town
□	Village
○	Large community

Map 24

But building new roads can lead to changes in the landscape in another way. When roads are built in an area, people become attracted to this area and build their homes there. One of the best examples of how new roads can attract housing is the area between Castries and Gros Islet.

1 Read again the section above about the road from Castries to Gros Islet. Write down how the landscape was changed as a result.
2 Look at the map opposite. Find the major roads marked on this map. Which towns and villages do they link?
3 Draw another map of our country showing the towns, villages and major roads. Mark on it the following man-made features:
a) The Vieux Fort Port;
b) Hewanorra Airport;
c) Point Seraphine;
d) Vigie Airport;
e) Pigeon Peninsula;
f) The Rodney Bay Marina.

OUR COUNTRY ST LUCIA
Below is the first verse of a song about our country. It was written by Linda Banks. The music was written by Joyce Auguste. The song is called Beautiful Isle.

BEAUTIFUL ISLE

Saint Lucia Helen of the West
Land of green hills by nature blessed
Steep mountains rising
From the sea and valleys spreading
Verdantly majestic Pitons Sulphur Springs
Saint Lucia land of beauteous things.

Linda Banks

Read the verse and answer the questions.

1 Why do you think St Lucia is called 'Helen of the West'?
2 What do the words 'green hills' and 'verdant valleys' suggest to us about our country?
3 Name the mountains which rise straight from the sea in our country.
4 What crop grows well in our verdant valleys?
5 In what ways are the Sulphur Springs important to our country?
6 Name four other beautiful things which nature gave to St Lucia.
7 How is St Lucia's beauty threatened? What can the citizens of our country do to keep it a 'Beautiful Isle' as the song suggests?

The people of our country

In *Caribbean Social Studies 3*, we thought about where our families came from. We found out whether our grandfathers and grandmothers were born here. We found that some of our families once came from Africa; some came from parts of Asia such as China and India. In our country and in the whole Caribbean region it is the same. People have come from all over the world to live here.

Indigenous peoples

Some of the families in our country have been here so long that we do not know exactly when they came. We call people like these *indigenous*. The indigenous peoples of the Caribbean are the Amerindians.

There were several groups of Amerindians in the Caribbean but as far as we know it was the Arawaks and later the Caribs, who lived in our country. You can see the kind of houses they lived in on page 28.

We know that Amerindians lived in our country because of the work of *archaeologists*. Archaeologists have found Amerindian remains or *artefacts* in several parts of our country, such as Choiseul, Soufriere, Vieux Fort, Dauphin, Grand Anse and Micoud. One of the biggest Amerindian sites was discovered by a group of archaeologists while digging along the eastern coast at a place called Pointe de Caille. They found a large number of stone axes, bits of pottery and many human skeletons.

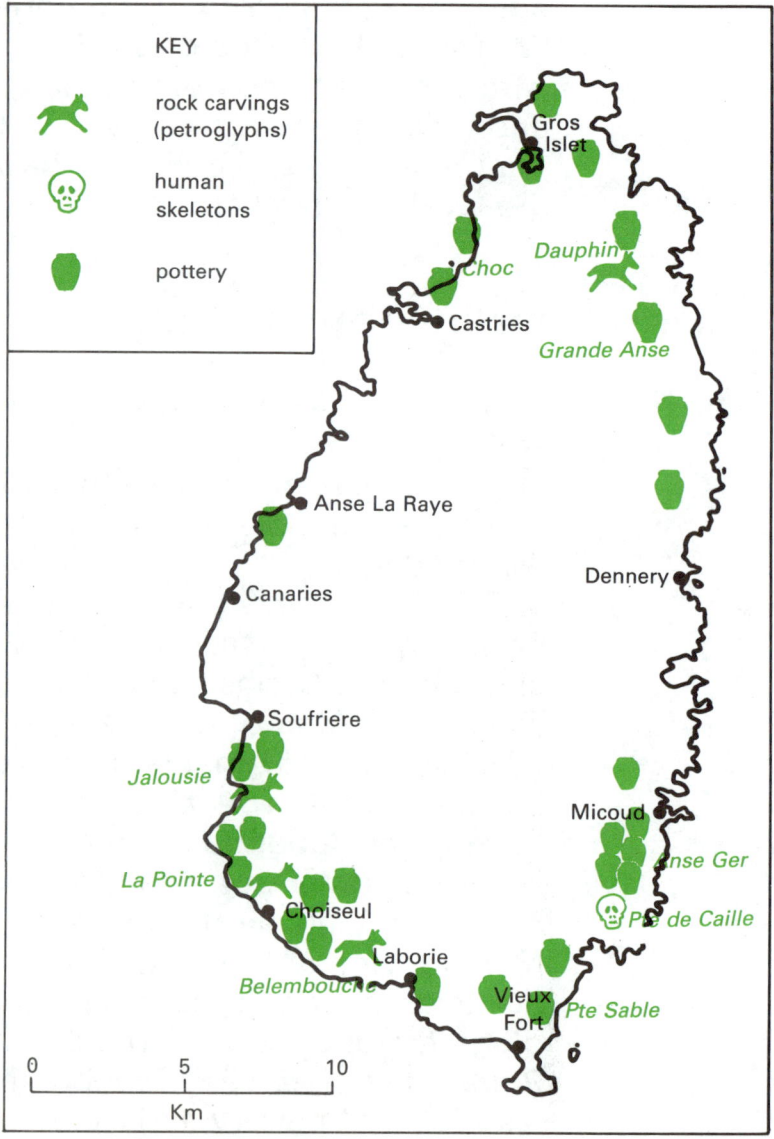

KEY

🦎 rock carvings (petroglyphs)

💀 human skeletons

▮ pottery

Gros Islet

Dauphin

Choc

Castries

Grande Anse

Anse La Raye

Canaries

Dennery

Soufriere

Jalousie

Micoud

La Pointe

Anse Ger

Choiseul

Pte de Caille

Laborie

Belembouche

Vieux Fort

Pte Sable

0   5   10
Km

Study the map showing Amerindian sites in St Lucia opposite. Is there a site near your school?

The Amerindians did not read and write as we do but they made special types of carvings, usually on pieces of rock, called **petroglyphs**. These rock carvings have been found at Dauphin, Soufriere and Choiseul. After studying petroglyphs, archaeologists can tell a great deal about the way people lived long ago.

Amerindians used fish bone as hooks, and also various types of nets for fishing. They also used bows and arrows. The Caribs were very good at shooting with bows and arrows. They travelled from island to island in the Caribbean by canoe.

Life in an Amerindian village

The Amerindians did not only fish in order to live. They were also farmers, who grew crops. Their main crop was cassava. After they had peeled and grated the cassava, they had a way of removing the poisonous juice from it. They made cassava bread as well as a drink from it. The Amerindians also grew corn, yams and beans for food and tobacco for smoking.

The Amerindians were very skilled craftsmen. They made very beautiful wood carvings. Their hammocks were very skilfully made out of cotton. Beautiful baskets were made with the various types of vines and grasses which grew in the *environment*. They made different types of pots out of the red clay soil.

Archaeologists believe that the Caribs painted their bodies before they went out on a raid. They did this in order to look fierce. Both Arawaks and Caribs painted their bodies when preparing for various ceremonies. In our country, the Amerindians used the reddish seeds of the roucou plant to paint their bodies as a form of protection from insect bites.

Both Arawak and Carib villages were headed by chiefs. These chiefs were in charge of all activities in their villages. The Arawak chiefs, called caciques, were very much respected. Arawaks believed that the chiefs could speak to their gods.

 Imagine you are an Amerindian. Write down a description of a day in your life. It might be an ordinary day or an important day. Draw a picture to go with your description.

Settlements in our country today

In *Caribbean Social Studies 2*, we learned about our community. We learned how it began, why people settled there, what kind of community it is.

We could study every community in this way. If we did that, we should find that many communities have similar *origins*. People settled there because it was easy to reach from nearby settlements, there was fresh water to drink, there was a way of earning a living by farming or fishing, and so on. Often new settlements were formed when there were too many people in one village. Some of the young people went to settle in another place not far away where there was more land available.

Most settlements began as rural ones, where there was local *employment*. People worked in jobs such as farming or fishing. Some settlements became towns because there was an important market or harbour there.

The settlement of Desruisseaux

Desruisseaux is one of the most rapidly developing settlements in our country. It is an **inland settlement** and part of the District of Micoud.

Desruisseaux

Find Desruisseaux on a map of St Lucia in your atlas. Describe its *location* in a sentence.

Like many other settlements in our country, the settlement of Desruisseaux got its name from a French family who owned a large amount of land in the area.

The settlement of Desruisseaux started as a number of small houses spread away from each other. Most of the people at that time worked on the estates in the area. As time went on, most of the large landowners began selling land to people. Those who could afford it bought land and started cultivating their own gardens. Desruisseaux therefore started as an *agricultural* settlement and agriculture is still the way in which most people earn a living.

Many of the people who settled in Desruisseaux once lived in the village of Micoud and other areas of the district. Some of those who lived in the village of Micoud walked distances of between five km and eight km (3–5 miles) to Desruisseaux almost daily to

31

tend their gardens. Others had two houses. They lived in Desruisseaux on weekdays but travelled to the village of Micoud on weekends to attend Church and other activities.

Look at the map of the Desruisseaux area. Use the scale line to measure the distance from Desruisseaux to Micoud.

At first there were hardly any modern *facilities* in the settlement of Desruisseaux. The people bought their goods in the village of Micoud or in Vieux Fort. There were no vehicles, so people often walked to Vieux Fort, carrying their loads on their heads for more than ten miles, to sell in the town. Although a small infant school was built earlier, children of primary school age had to walk to the village of Micoud until 1959, when the Desruisseaux Combined School opened.

Until the 1960s there were no **public services** such as electricity, pipe water, or telephones in the settlement. The residents had to walk distances of about one kilometre in some cases to collect water for drinking from the river, ravines or springs. At that time water was carried mainly in calabashes and stored at home in large earthern pots. Most of the washing was done in the river or the ravines. On wash days, the children loved to play and fish in the rivers while their parents washed the clothes. On dark nights, the people found their way along the tracks to and from their homes with lighted flambeaux or **'shalls'**.

Over the years the community has changed. Now there are many lovely houses and they are much closer to each other. There are many services such as schools, churches, pipe water, electricity, telephones, shops, supermarkets and petrol stations. The people no longer have to depend on the Village of Micoud for their everyday needs.

There are more than 3000 people living in the settlement of Desruisseaux now. They no longer have to carry heavy loads over great distances or depend on donkeys as they used to do before. Many of the

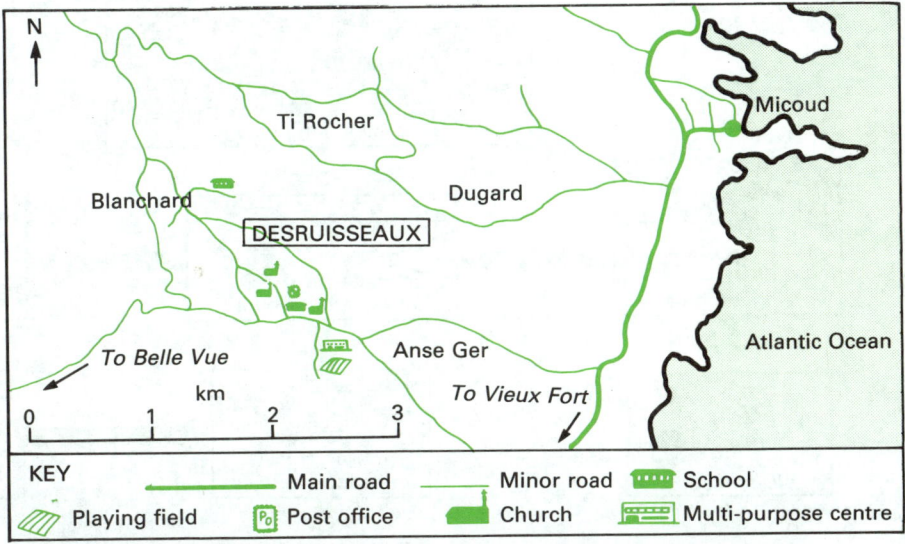

Desruisseaux and neighbouring communities

people of Desruisseaux own vehicles. Travel to other communities has become much easier and quicker. There are many community organisations which are all trying to improve the community.

Use the map of the Desruisseaux area to answer the following questions:

1 Name the neighbouring communities around Desruisseaux.
2 Make a list of the facilities which Desruisseaux has today.
3 To which major.towns and villages is it easy to travel from Desruisseaux?
4 Is Desruisseaux on the coast? What do we call a settlement in this location?

How a community grows

A flow chart is a picture which shows us how things happen. It shows how one event leads to another event. Look at the flow chart on page 34. It shows how a settlement grew. This community began as a fishing community in a small village. Then a new harbour is built so that larger ships can come there. . . .

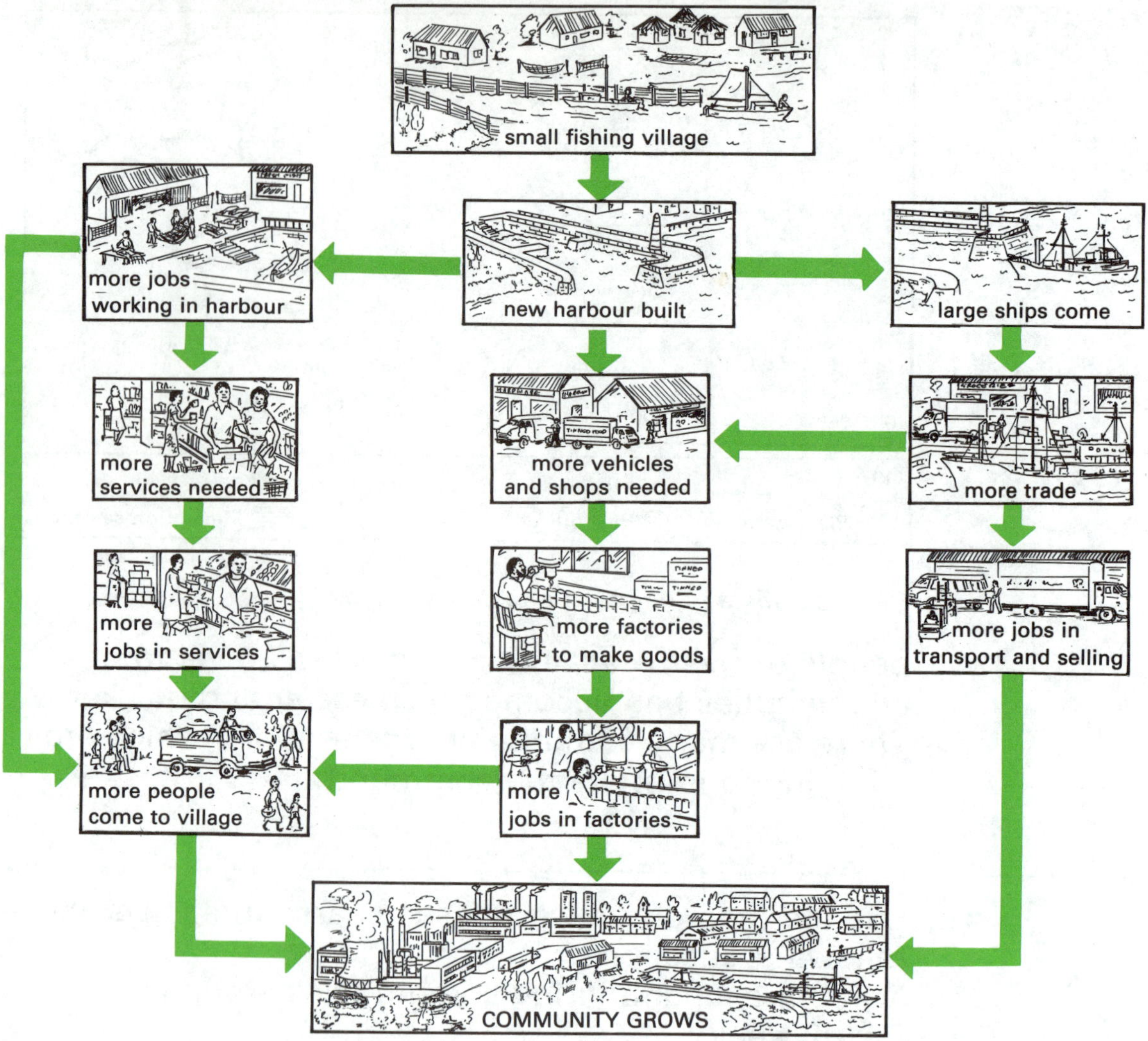

The following are part of the flow chart illustration:

small fishing village

new harbour built → **more jobs working in harbour** / **large ships come**

more services needed

more vehicles and shops needed

more trade

more jobs in services

more factories to make goods

more jobs in transport and selling

more people come to village

more jobs in factories

COMMUNITY GROWS

Compare the growth of this community with the way Desruisseaux grew. Draw a flow chart to show the growth of Desruisseaux. Was a deep harbour important in the development of Desruisseaux?

Problems

Large settlements sometimes have **social problems**. They may become overcrowded; there is not enough work for everyone; people may become involved with drugs or illegal activities. When settlements become

What effects do housing estates like this one have on a community?

overcrowded people are often forced to *squat* on any bit of land that they can find. They often build small shacks using any bit of wood, cardboard or even tin, that they can find. Very often these areas have no piped water or electricity and sanitation is often poor. In our country and in many other countries in the Caribbean, such housing areas are called **shanty towns**.

Many of the people who live in these poor areas do not work. They therefore remain idle and this often leads to other problems such as stealing, gambling and taking illegal drugs. Taking drugs is a very dangerous practice. Not only do drugs affect the health of those who use them, but drug users often steal to find money to buy the drugs. Many young boys and girls are caught in this unfortunate situation.

Not all children from shanty towns or from poor communities get involved in stealing and drugs. Some of them, although they are poor, are determined to become successful and good citizens. They therefore try their best in school and many of them do succeed. Some of these are able not only to improve the way they live, but also to help other less fortunate members of their families.

Population

When we speak of the **population** of a place we mean the people who live in that place. If for example, we ask what the population of Anse La Raye is, we are in fact trying to find out the total number of people living in the part of our country called Anse La Raye. The population of St Lucia is the total number of people who live in our country. Table 1 (page 14) gives the estimated number of people living in St Lucia in 1990.

More people live in some parts of our country than in others. Some districts have larger populations than others. The map shows the districts of St Lucia.

1 Look at Table 2 on page 37. It shows the population for the districts in St Lucia in 1990 and 1998. Name the three districts which have the largest populations.
2 Which district had the biggest increase in population between 1990 and 1998?
3 Which district had the smallest increase in population between 1990 and 1998?
4 Did the population decrease between 1990 and 1998?

In some districts the people are spread all over the area in many small communities. The district of Choiseul is an example of such a district. Some other districts have fewer communities, but with much larger populations. The district of Micoud is like this. There are only about twelve communities in the district of Micoud, but it has a population more than twice as big as Choiseul. Yet the district of Choiseul is made up of over 20 communities – almost twice the number of communities which the district of Micoud has!

The people of our country do not all remain in the same district in which they were born. People leave their districts and settle in others for various reasons.

Were you born in the district in which you now live? Were your mother and father born in the district in which they live now? If they were not born there ask them why they moved to another district.

Table 2 Population of districts of St Lucia: 1990 and 1998 (Figures given to the nearest 100)

District	1990	1998
Anse La Raye	5 100	6 100
Canaries	1 800	1 900
Castries	52 300	60 900
Choiseul	6 400	7 100
Dennery	11 200	12 600
Gros Islet	13 500	14 000
Laborie	7 500	8 600
Micoud	15 200	17 200
Soufriere	7 700	8 900
Vieux Fort	13 200	14 400

Culture

The *culture* of a group of people means how they live, what language they speak and how they speak it; what clothes they wear; what food they eat and how they prepare it; what types of celebrations and traditions they have and even what games they play.

All the different groups of people who came to our country have played their part in forming our culture. In some cases we still practise some things in much the same way as the people who invented them. For example, we play cricket and football in much the same way as the Europeans. In other cases we have mixed the practices of several groups to form our own. One good example of this mixture is what we call *Creole*: we have combined English, French and African ways of speaking to form a new language.

Each statement on the left is linked to a word on the right.

Copy the list below in your notebook. Draw lines joining the statements on the left to the matching place or people on the right.

1 They introduced the English language to our country.
2 St Lucians make drums with animal skin.
3 Many St Lucians like Jazz Music.
4 Most places in St Lucia were named by them.
5 Cassava was first cultivated by them.
6 On formal occasions we wear jacket and tie.
7 Roti is popular in St Lucia.

INDIAN
FRANCE
BRITAIN
UNITED STATES
OF AMERICA
EUROPE
AMERINDIAN
AFRICA

We have seen that the mixture of different people in our country gives us our culture – traditional customs, festival, food, literature, art and music.

Some of our culture is shared with other countries in the Caribbean; some of it is only found here.

Christmas

Christmas is a festival which is celebrated in all the Caribbean islands. This is because Christmas is a Christian feast and there are many Christians in the Caribbean islands. In our country although they belong to different churches, almost all the people are Christians. Over three-quarters of the people of our country are Roman Catholics.

Roman Catholics celebrate the birth of Jesus Christ on 25 December. The 'Christmas season' actually begins many days before Christmas Day. People begin to clean and decorate their homes. They also buy large amounts of food and drink. Many buy new furniture and clothes for themselves and their families. Children are given new toys and the radio stations play Christmas carols. In some of the rural communities you may hear the sounds of bamboo cannons.

At about midnight on 24 December, the traditional 'midnight mass' is held so that the people can mark the birth of Christ. It is common for Christmas parties to begin after midnight mass is over. During the rest of the season, people visit friends, exchange gifts and attend parties and fairs. During these activities there is much eating and drinking.

In our country, the season lasts until the day after the New Year. On these last two days, many people travel to Castries to attend the traditional New Year's Day Fair.

National Day

Most countries have special days which are important to the people. In some cases it is the birthday of a great leader. In others, it may be the date on which something very important to the people took place.

In our country, 13 December is celebrated as our **National Day**. It was once believed that Christopher Columbus saw our country for the first time on

13 December. Most of our people do not believe this any more but 13 December remains as our national day. This day is also a big feast day for the Roman Catholic Church. It is the date when Catholics in our country mark the feast of Saint Lucy who is the Patron Saint of Saint Lucia.

During National Day celebrations, the people in the various communities organise and take part in various types of activities. There are church services, youth rallies, singing, dancing, sporting and other cultural activities. One of the most popular events which people look forward to seeing is the 'Festival of Lights'.

Independence

Another important date for the people of our country is 22 February. It was on this day in 1979 that our country became independent. Every year we celebrate the anniversary of our independence on 22 February.

We celebrate the anniversary of our independence in much the same way that we celebrate our National Day. For example, the celebrations begin many days before 22 February. Many schoolchildren look forward to being selected to represent their schools at the big independence anniversary rally which is held in Castries. During the rally the people listen to speeches from important people in the country, such as the Prime Minister and other members of government. They also sing patriotic songs.

La Rose and La Marguerite

La Rose and La Marguerite are two flower festivals. La Rose is celebrated on 30 August and La Marguerite on 17 October. In both festivals the people who take part dress in the kind of clothes worn by Europeans when they ruled in the Caribbean. There are a king, queen, doctors, nurses, soldiers and common people. During their celebrations both groups use traditional instruments such as the violin, shac-shac, banjo and drum.

There are some differences between the festivals.

La Rose

La Marguerite

Which flower festival is being celebrated here?

The La Rose groups have the rose flower as their symbol and during their celebrations they dress in red. La Marguerite groups, on the other hand, have the blueish marguerite flower as their symbol. They dress in blue. You can see the flower symbols in the picture.

On the day of their celebrations the groups first attend church service and afterwards parade the streets in their communities. Sometimes, groups gather at a special venue where they perform. During their celebrations, the La Rose and La Marguerite sing songs praising their flower, or their king. However, the words of some of their songs are chosen to make fun of each other. This friendly rivalry between the La Rose and La Marguerite may be a very thoughtful way of *dramatising* the real rivalries which took place between the English and the French a few hundred years ago.

Carnival

Many Caribbean countries celebrate Carnival, but not all of them do so at the same time. Some countries, such as

Some Caribbean countries have changed the dates of their Carnival celebrations to July or August.

Trinidad and Tobago and Dominica continue to celebrate on the days just before Ash Wednesday each year.

Preparations begin long before the celebrations. Carnival bands design and construct costumes. Calypsonians begin singing in the 'tents' in preparation for the big Calypso King or Queen competition, and young ladies prepare for the Carnival Queen competition.

In all cases, celebrations begin with a street 'jump up' called Jour Ouvert, and another jump up called Last Lap on Tuesday evening after the parade of bands and prize-giving ceremonies are over.

Name three Caribbean countries that do not celebrate Carnival on the Monday and Tuesday before Ash Wednesday.

Jounen Kweyol

In October one date has become important in our country. This is 28 October: the day when all countries which speak Creole mark Creole Day, (Jounen Kweyol).

Jounen Kweyol is celebrated in our country on the Sunday which is closest to 28 October. The purpose of the celebration is to help the people to see the importance of our Creole in the development of our country.

Each year the organisers of the celebrations name the communities where the activities will be held. The activities always begin with a religious service in Creole. This is usually followed by activities such as honouring people who have contributed to the development of Creole, and cooking and eating traditional foods.

People really enjoy the music and dancing. The younger people are encouraged to learn as they watch the older folk dance traditional dances such as the quadrille.

Speak to people in your community about Carnival. Find out from them what things they like about the event and what things they do not like about it. Make your notes as you speak to them.

When you have finished, write an account of about two paragraphs stating what the people in your interview liked and disliked about Carnival.

A CROSSWORD PUZZLE

Copy this crossword puzzle and fill in the missing letters. The answers are in the clues given below.

¹C	²A			Q		E		³C		
	R			⁴R				⁵L		⁶ Y
⁷	O		C		U					A	
								⁸B		N
			E							
⁹M					¹⁰S				E	
					H		H			
¹¹C		S	S	V						¹²W
					L					
U				¹³	I		H		S	
¹⁴	O		K		Y					

ACROSS
1. The name given to an Arawak chief.
5. The Patron Saint of St Lucia.
7. The Amerindians used it to protect themselves from insect bites.
8. Used by the Amerindians for fish hooks.
11. The Amerindians' chief crop.
13. During National Day activities we have the Festival of . . .
14. Long ago farmers used it for transport.

DOWN
2. The Amerindians used it for hunting, fishing and fighting.
3. Long ago this fruit was used to collect water.
4. On 30 August, we often hear "Vive La . . . ."
6. Sea transport for the Amerindians.
9. The community of Desruisseaux at one time had close links with the village of . . . .
10. Ancient type of lighted torch.
12. Many people still use the river to . . . .

Our natural resources

Do you remember the word *resources*? What does it mean? If you do not know, look it up in the glossary on page 107 and find out.

In our country we have many kinds of resources. We can divide these into two main groups – *renewable* resources and *non-renewable* resources.

Renewable resources

These are resources which do not run out. The natural world restores them if it is allowed to do so. For example, animals and plants are renewable resources. They grow and reproduce so that they are always available to us. But if we destroy all the animal and plant life in the area it will take a long time to renew.

Water and soil
Plants need water and soil to grow. Animals need water and food in order to live.

The main source of fresh water in our country is rain. When rain falls water seeps into the ground. If enough rain falls, this water forms streams and then rivers. Most of the rain in our country falls in the hills and mountains in the central part of the island.

Using rainfall data
When we measure rainfall, we record the *data* carefully. Table 3 shows **average** rainfall data for each month for the town of Castries. This means that this

is the normal rainfall for each month, recorded over many years. The rainfall graph below shows these figures in a diagram.

The map shows the pattern of rainfall over the whole of St Lucia. The winds blow from the north-east. They rise up over the mountains, carrying the clouds with them, and the clouds drop most of their rain on the mountains and hills in the centre of the island.

1 Study the graph, the rainfall map and Table 3 carefully. Use the information you find in them to answer these questions.
 a) During which month does the most rain fall?
 b) Which month is normally the driest?
 c) During which months would you say that our country has its rainy season?
2 Draw a bar chart showing the monthly rainfall records for your weather station over the past year.

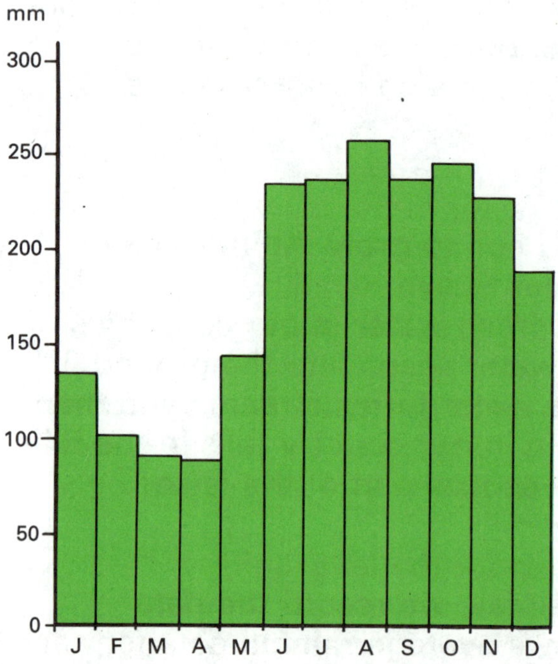

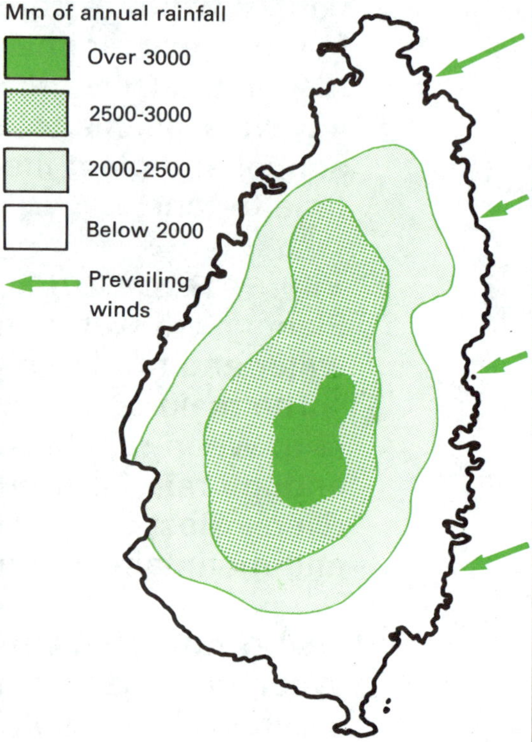

mm

Mm of annual rainfall

Over 3000

2500-3000

2000-2500

Below 2000

Prevailing winds

Table 3 Rainfall figures for Castries (mm)

J	F	M	A	M	J	J	A	S	O	N	D
137	101	91	89	145	234	236	259	236	244	226	188

Soil erosion

Our soils need water in order to make them *fertile* so that plants can grow well. In the parts of our country where very little rain falls, we find very few large trees. The plants which grow in these areas are those which can survive in very dry lands.

Although soils need water to make them fertile, water can destroy soils. Rain water can cause *soil erosion*. When heavy rain falls and the droplets of water fall directly on the land, particles of soil become loose. If this happens on a steep slope the top soil is washed away. If it rains for a long time, this soil eventually enters streams and rivers, which wash it into the sea.

In our country this has become a serious problem. People cut trees without thinking or caring about the results of their actions. Trees are very important. Their roots help to keep the soil together. The branches and leaves of trees prevent rain water from falling with great force on to the ground. Where there are many large trees, water remains in the ground much longer and the rivers will always have water. But because many trees have been cut in the forest some streams and even rivers dry up during the dry season.

There are many places in our country where there was once a lot of soil and large trees. But as people cut the trees water washed the soil away until only the bare rock remained.

It is useful to learn about the local soil by experimenting. The Soil and Water Survey on page 48 will help you to find out more about the soil in the area where you live.

SOIL AND WATER SURVEY

Your teacher will help you carry out the instructions for this survey.

1 Find out where the people of your community get their water. Begin by finding out where the water comes from which you use in your home and at school. Are these sources different? Compare notes with the other members of your class. Do you all get your water from the same source? Write down your findings.

2 Work in small groups. Each group will study the soil in a part of your local area. Your teacher will help you to organise this. Each group will go out into the community and come back with a **soil sample**. You can dig up a spoonful of soil and put it in a jar. Compare the jar of soil with soil which another group has collected. Do they all look the same?

3 Do some experiments with your soil at school. For example, you can crumble the dry soil in your hand. Some soil is very crumbly and soft. Other soils are lumpy and hard when they are dry. Try some other experiments with the soil. Try some using water. Write down what you find out. Is all the soil in your community the same kind of soil, or not?

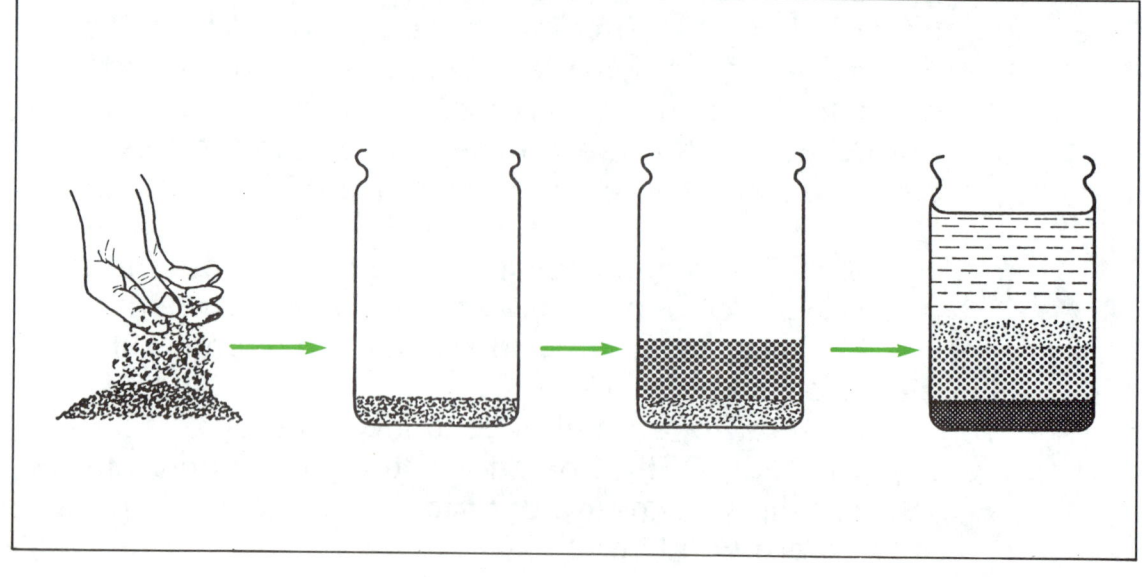

The forests are important

The resources of our country are important to us. We must therefore use them carefully and wisely, even those which are renewable. Because we have been careless in the past we have caused damage to many of our resources. The forest is one example. Because the forest is so important to us the Forestry Department of our country chose as its motto: 'La Foway say la Vie'. In English this means 'The Forest is Life'.

Long ago, before people used gas for cooking, charcoal was the main source of fuel. People cut trees for making charcoal and also to make boards and posts to build their homes. These practices did not seem to cause much damage to the forest because the population was small. But as more and more trees were cut, the forest began to suffer. As time went on more and more people cut trees to cultivate bananas. The problem got worse. By 1970, the problem had become so serious that the government had to act in order to prevent all the forest being destroyed.

At the present time, over 72 sq km (18 000 acres) has been declared a **forest reserve**. No one is allowed to cut trees in this area. The Forestry Department has replanted many trees in an effort to maintain the forest. In order to help people who earn a living by producing charcoal, the Forestry Department is planting some types of trees which grow very quickly. Leucaenia is one of these.

It is not only the forest which is in danger. Some of our country's animals came close to disappearing. The one which caused the greatest amount of concern was our National Bird – the Parrot. If the forest is destroyed, the parrots will lose the trees which provide them with food, and a place for making their nests. It is not only the forest which is protected by law. It is an offence to kill any wild animal except the poisonous Fer de Lance snake. You will see that there is a very close link between the forest, our wild animals and our supply of water. If the forest is destroyed, the others will also be affected and will perhaps disappear.

 ■ ■ Look carefully at the photograph on page 49. Then answer the questions.

1 Give two reasons why trees are cut down.
2 In which group of resources would you place trees, renewable or non-renewable?
3 Why is it important to plan our tree-cutting? What can happen if we remove forest trees without proper planning?
4 What is being done in our country to plant new trees?

Sand from the beaches
Long ago most of the houses built in our country were made out of wood. This is not so any more. Most of the houses being built new are made out of concrete. People therefore need sand for building.

They have removed sand from the beaches at such a rapid rate that the sea cannot replace the sand quickly enough. The result is that some beaches have been destroyed already, and others are in danger of being destroyed. It is important that people understand the importance of protecting our country's beaches. If the beach is destroyed, people will not be able to enjoy themselves there. It will also become easier for the sea to come in and wash away the land.

Non-renewable resources

These resources will not restore themselves. This means that they will not always be available. They have taken many thousand of years to be made. If we use them too quickly they will soon run out.

Some Caribbean countries have valuable non-renewable resources such as petroleum, bauxite, limestone and gold. You will learn more about these in *Caribbean Social Studies 5*. In St Lucia we do not have many non-renewable resources like these. Our economy depends on our agriculture and fishing.

Using our resources

Our country has two very important needs. Firstly we need to provide as many jobs as possible for the people. Secondly, we need to be able to make money to pay for the things which we buy from other countries. In order to do this, our country must try to develop as many industries as possible. We must develop agriculture and tourism more. We must also develop *manufacturing industry*.

We use our animals and plant resources in two ways. One way is to farm and fish only for our own food. This is called *subsistence*. This is how the Amerindians who were here long ago used resources. Another way is to farm and fish in order to sell what we produce. This is called *commercial* agriculture and fishing.

Making a living in Choiseul

The village of Choiseul is located on the south-western coast of St Lucia. Although the village is small, with a population of about 2000 people, there are many other communities forming the district. Sometimes it is difficult to know where some communities begin and others end. They seem to merge into one another.

Most of the people in the village of Choiseul make a livelihood through fishing. Choiseul can therefore be called a fishing village. The district is also very

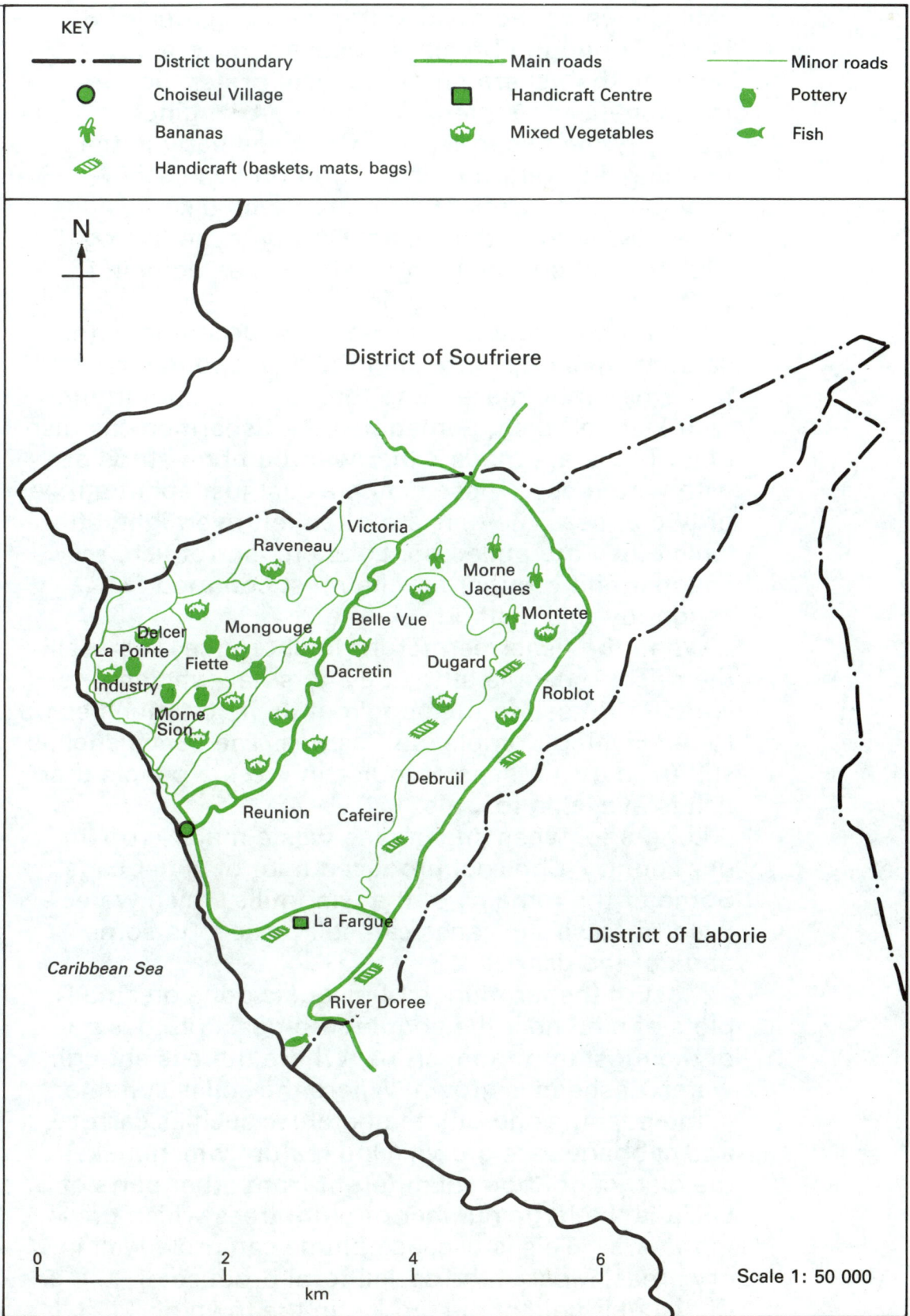

well known as the main craft-producing area of St Lucia. Although fibreglass boats are becoming popular, the fishermen of Choiseul prefer the traditional canoe fitted with outboard engines. Normally the fishermen go out to sea early in the morning and return in the afternoon. On such a fishing trip, they might go more than 80 km (50 miles) away from the island. During these fishing trips they often catch large fish such as dolphin fish, yellow-fin tuna, and king fish.

During the months of November, December and January, flying fish are plentiful. On a good day, the fishermen may make more than two trips returning with loaded boats. Sometimes the fishermen cast fish pots. These are made either with bamboo strips or with wire mesh. These nets are cast just about a mile or two at sea. The nets are often left overnight, after which they are pulled up. Lobsters, parrot fish, red snapper and grouper are the most common fish caught by this method.

When the fishermen return to shore they may sell their fish to people at the bay, to small wholesalers who in turn sell to the people of their communities or to the Fishing Complex in Castries. The conch shell is still used as a means of indicating to the people that fish is available for sale.

Long ago, when sugar cane was a major crop in our country, Choiseul produced a lot of sugar cane. Some of the remains of the windmills which were used to crush the canes can still be seen in some parts of the district.

Most of the farming in Choiseul is done on small plots of land near the people's homes. Potato is one of the most important crops. Where there is enough water, dasheen is grown. Where the soil is suitable, some peanuts and other vegetables such as carrots and cabbages are grown. One feature which makes the district of Choiseul different from other parts of St Lucia is the large number of plum trees which grow in the area. This is because plums can grow well in dry areas. Most of the agricultural produce of Choiseul is sold at the market in the town of

Vieux Fort on Fridays and Saturdays.

The district of Choiseul is very well known for the making of crafts. In some communities, such as Caffiere, Debrieul and Roblot, the people specialise in weaving, making such items as mats, bags, baskets and chairs. Pottery is carried out in the western part of the district in places such as La Pointe, Morne Sion, Fiette and Delcer. Most of the *raw materials* are obtained locally. The potters use clay while the weavers use various types of grass and vines such as screwpine, sisal, khus khus and wicker.

There is a Craft Centre at La Fargue where people make and also put their crafts on display for sale. This centre is visited often by tourists as well as local people. Many of the crafts are sold in Castries, Vieux Fort and Soufrière. The act of pottery and weaving was handed down among generations of Choiseulians from the time of the Amerindians.

1 Make a study of your own district like this study of Choiseul. Use the questions in the box on page 56 and the photographs to help you. If you live in Choiseul district, you may wish to try and visit the places where people carry on the activities mentioned on pages 52-55. Do you or your family take part in any of these activities?

2 Look carefully at the map of Choiseul district on page 53. (Look back at the map of the districts of St Lucia on page 37 to see where the district of Choiseul is.) Find the handicraft centre, the potteries and the fishing areas. Trace the route of the main roads. Which communities do they link?

How do people make their living in your district? Do they fish, grow bananas or vegetables, or make crafts? What else do they do to earn a living?

What kind of boats do people in your district use for fishing? What other methods of fishing do they use?

What vegetables do people in your district grow? Where do they sell them?

Mending the nets

56

Fishing boats in Castries harbour

The Saturday market in Castries – what is being sold here?

What is being grown in this field?

Manufacturing in St Lucia

Manufacturing in St Lucia started with the processing of agricultural products such as sugar cane into sugar and rum, and copra into cooking oil. Later other industries such as bay rum, soft drinks and furniture were added.

During the 1960s the government realised that because of the growing population there would be need to provide many more jobs. They therefore decided to encourage the development of manufacturing industries. By 1975, many new manufacturing industries had been established. These included the Heineken Brewery and the Winera box-making factory in Vieux Fort and the Mayfair garment factory in Castries. The government has selected special areas where factories can be established. These areas are called industrial estates. By 1991, there were industrial estates at Bisee, Choc, Gros Islet, Odsan, Dennery and Vieux Fort. You can see one in the photograph.

St Lucia now has manufacturing industries making beverages, furniture, boxes, plastic products, cooking oil, margarine, clothing and various types of building materials and household items.

Make a list of things which are manufactured in our country. Are any of these manufacturing industries located in your district?

Human resources

For agriculture, fishing and industry, we need the work of human beings. Their work is called *human resources*. We also use our human resources to provide **services** for us. These services make it easier for everyone to live better. There are several different groups of people who provide services in our country. The police, sanitation workers, fire officers, postal workers, janitors, watchmen, market vendors and teachers are some of them.

How are human resources being used in the photograph? Can you think of other persons whose work serves as a human resource?

How are human resources being used here?

Work of the meteorologist

When we listen to the radio, there are certain times each day when the announcer presents the **'weather report'**. This report is a statement about what the weather is like and what changes are likely to take place during the next 24 hours.

The weather report is usually prepared at the Meteorological Office near the Hewanorra Airport in Vieux Fort. The people who study the weather patterns are called meteorologists. Sometimes, people simply call them 'Met Officers'. The service which the met officers provide for the public is very important. The weather reports provide valuable information to people, and help them to plan their activities. For example, a farmer who uses chemicals which are affected by rain might have to postpone their use if the weather report states that it will rain heavily during the day.

People have learned to pay close attention to the weather report during the hurricane season. With the

A weather satellite photograph shows a hurricane brewing in the Caribbean

help of satellite pictures taken from above the earth the met officers can explain quite clearly to us, on television, what the weather is likely to be like for several days. They can also give us very accurate information about storms and hurricanes. They can tell us when and where a hurricane is developing, and even the direction in, or speed at, which they are moving. With this information we can take action to reduce damage and injury to ourselves and families.

Some of the people who provide services for everyone work for the government. But many do not. Some work in shops, stores and airline offices. Others are employed as insurance agents and bank clerks. The work of all of them is important. They all help to provide us with the things we need.

 Read this account of Nurse Leslie's work at Mon Repos Health Centre. Find out about the work of a nurse at your local health centre.

The work of a nurse

I am Nurse Leslie. I work at the Mon Repos Health Centre. My job is to help those who are sick to return to good health and to help others remain healthy.

On normal days, I do several things such as:
- helping people to find out if they are **diabetics**;
- advising people on their eating habits;
- checking people's **blood pressure**;
- examining pregnant mothers to ensure that they and the unborn babies are well;
- examining mothers and their young babies to ensure that they are healthy;
- advising young mothers on the need to plan their families;
- holding meetings with groups of people suffering from diabetes and **hypertension**.

Find out what the words in bold print mean.

The doctor visits our health centre on Wednesdays. This is a busy day for me. On Wednesdays I have to see that the patients visit the doctor in an orderly manner. I also help the

pharmacist in helping the people to understand how to take their medicines properly.

Sometimes I have to visit schools to talk to the pupils and teachers on certain health matters.

 Draw a table showing areas of work where people provide services as part of their job. State whether they are public servants, (that is, they work for the government), or whether they work in private business. In the last column, say how human resources are used in this job. We have started the table for you.

Table 4 Using human resources

Activity	Public or private	Human resources
Farming	Private	Working in the fields; caring for animals; selling food
Teaching	Public	

PICTURE WORK

Study this photograph of Soufriere carefully and answer these questions.

1 Where do you think the picture was taken from?
2 Describe what you can see in the picture.
3 List the resources you can see used in the picture, under the headings *Renewable resources*, and *Non-renewable resources*.
4 In what ways have human resources been used to create what you can see in the picture?
5 What are the dangers to our environment? Can you see any of these dangers in the photograph?

TOPIC 4

Tourism and trade

Tourists

Write down what you think the word **tourist** means. What is a tourist?

When we think about what a word means, we *define* it. The definition of a tourist tells us what a tourist is. We could define tourists like this:

Tourists are people who come from another country to our country to enjoy themselves.

Can you think of a better definition? Write down your own definition of tourists.

Tourists come to our country on holiday or for business. They stay here for a few days or weeks. Then they go home again. At home they work hard to earn money just as we do. Most of the tourists who come to our country live in hotels during their visits.

Tourist attractions
Historic sites and buildings, beautiful beaches, hills, waterfalls, and of course the Sulphur Springs, are all important tourist attractions in our country.

The photographs on page 65 show some tourist attractions around the town of Soufriere. Can you say what each attraction is? Why do you think tourists visit these attractions?

64

Let's meet Cox

Cox works in a hotel. He is one of the many workers at the hotel who helps the tourists enjoy their holiday. Cox works in the sports department of the hotel. His job is to assist the tourists who want to go horseback riding.

On a normal day, Cox reaches the hotel at seven in the morning. His first task is to go to the stables where the horses are kept. By that time, the horses have been fed by a co-worker who came in two hours before him. Each horse has a name. Cox grooms the horses by brushing them and removing any bits of wood shaving which might cling to their bodies. He then gets the horses ready for the guests to go horseback riding. A special saddle is used for beginners. The route which the tourists follow when riding is called the trail. Either Cox or one of his friends who works in the stables always accompanies the tourists when they go on the trail.

65

At about ten o'clock, the horses are returned to the stables for lunch. Then about two hours later they all receive a shower. They are ready to go on another trail at about three o'clock. When there are not many tourists who wish to go horseback riding, Cox and his friends have to go out with the horses to exercise them.

At about six o'clock, all horses are taken to their stables. There they are inspected for injury or damaged shoes. Whatever is discovered is recorded so that on the following day the injury or damage can be put right. Cox likes his work because he likes horses. He also likes to see the visitors enjoying their riding.

On most days Cox works from seven o'clock to two-thirty but sometimes he works on the ten o'clock to six o'clock shift.

Imagine that you are Cox or one of the other workers in the hotel where he works. Write a diary for a week. Imagine the people he meets, the things that go well (or badly) and how he feels about his work. Draw some pictures to illustrate your work.

The tourist industry

In Unit 3 we learned about manufacturing industry. We call the work we do to look after tourists, the **tourist industry**. Cox works in the tourist industry. Many tourists come to the Caribbean on holiday each year.

The tourist industry is very important to our country in several ways. When the tourists come to our country, they stay in hotels. The hotels employ many people so that they can provide the tourists with everything they want, such as food and entertainment.

Many other people who do not work at the hotels also benefit from the tourist industry. Can you think of some non-hotel workers who benefit from tourism? The pictures may help you.

Cruise visitors

Not all visitors are stay-over visitors. Many are **cruise visitors** or *cruise-ship passengers*. This means that they visit in cruise ships or in yachts like those shown on page 66. Every week cruise ships come into Port Castries, especially near Point Seraphine. These visitors spend a number of hours visiting the country. Then they return to their ship and sail to another country. In this way they are able to visit many islands during their cruise.

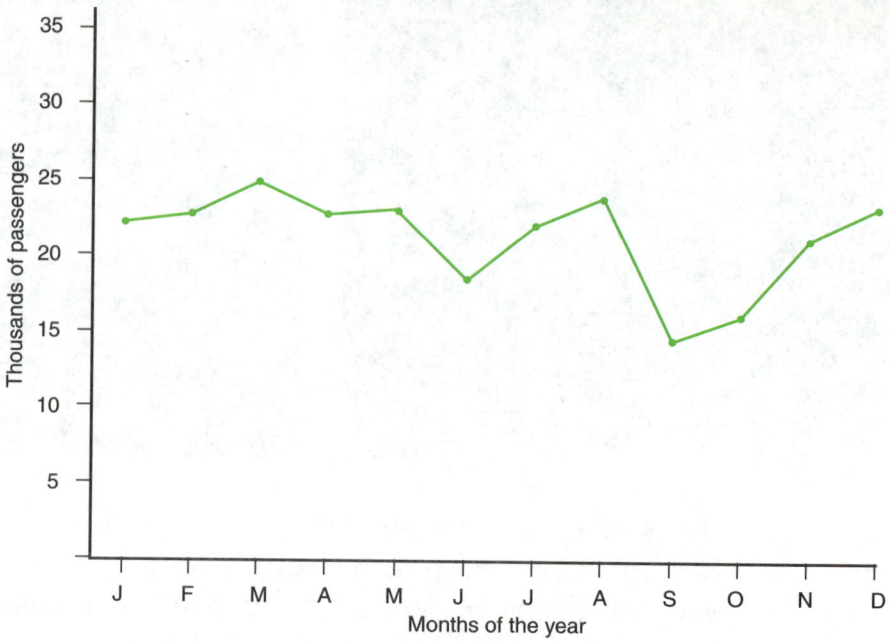

Visitor arrivals to St Lucia by month, 1998

 Study the graph showing visitor arrivals to St Lucia in 1998. Use information presented in the graph to answer the following questions.

a) In which month did most visitors come to St Lucia?

b) In which month did the least numbers of visitors arrive?

c) Does this graph suggest there is a 'tourist season' in St Lucia? Why do you think so?

d) Describe the way the numbers of visitors changed in 1998. You can begin this way, 'In January more than 22 000 tourists visited St Lucia...'

Where do the tourists come from?

Tourists come to St Lucia from many places in the world. Some come from Europe, others come from North America, South America and other parts of the Caribbean. Tourists who come from other parts of the Caribbean are known as **Caribbean tourists**.

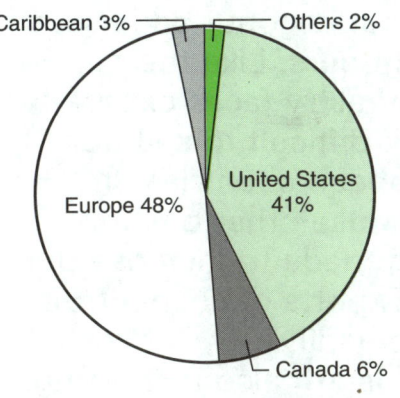

Caribbean 3% — ⌐ Others 2%

Europe 48%

United States 41%

Canada 6%

Source: St Lucia Tourist Board, 1999

Look at the pie chart showing the numbers of tourists from different places for the year 1999. From which area did most tourists come? What do the words 'not stated' mean?

Trade

Tourism brings money into our country. Tourists buy our goods and create jobs for our people in hotels, airports and elsewhere.

Our country also earns money by **trade**. Trading involves buying and selling goods and services. When we trade with other Countries we talk about **exports** and **imports**.

Exports

Exports are goods which are made in our country and sold to people in other countries. The main agricultural exports of our country are bananas and coconut oil. These products have earned a great deal of money for our country. The main *market* for our bananas is the United Kingdom. But the people of the United Kingdom do not like the fruit when they look ugly. It becomes difficult to sell such poor-quality fruit especially when there are other bananas which look better than ours.

When the quality of the bananas is poor, the price drops and the farmers in our country get less money for their bananas. In order to keep the price of our bananas high, we must try to sell good-quality fruit. Despite these problems, bananas have earned many millions of dollars for our farmers. Our farmers also grow large numbers of coconuts. Dry coconuts are made into copra. This is used to make coconut oil at

69

a factory in Soufriere. Most of our coconut oil is sold to some of our Caribbean neighbours. Like the banana industry, the coconut industry faces export problems sometimes. We find it difficult to sell our coconut oil, even to other Caribbean countries. In some countries people prefer to use other oils for cooking. Great efforts are being made to increase our country's agricultural exports. Exports of cocoa, fruit and vegetables are increasing steadily.

Exports of manufactured goods are also increasing. One of our main exports of manufactured goods is *beverages* such as beer and malt. These are produced at a factory in Vieux Fort. We also export large amounts of clothing and cardboard boxes.

Imports

As well as selling goods abroad, we also buy many goods from other countries. These are called **imports**. It would not be possible to make a list here of all the things which we import. These are some of the most common ones — food, clothing, vehicles, medicines, building materials and home appliances. We import our goods from many different countries in the Caribbean as well as other countries of the world, but we buy much more from some than from others.

Study the table and graph showing the value of St Lucia's imports and exports for the years 1985 to 1990. Answer the following questions.

1 In which year was the value of exports the highest?
2 What was the total value of St Lucia's exports in 1985?
3 Name one year in which the value of exports dropped from the previous year.
4 What was the value of St Lucia's imports in 1990?
5 In which year was there the biggest difference between the value of St Lucia's imports and the value of her exports?
6 In what way are the figures for 1990 different from the others?

Table 5 Imports and exports 1994–98

Year	Value of imports (million EC dollars)	Value of exports (million EC dollars)
1994	816.6	254.7
1995	826.5	294.2
1996	845.9	214.8
1997	897.0	165.4
1998	905.1	167.16

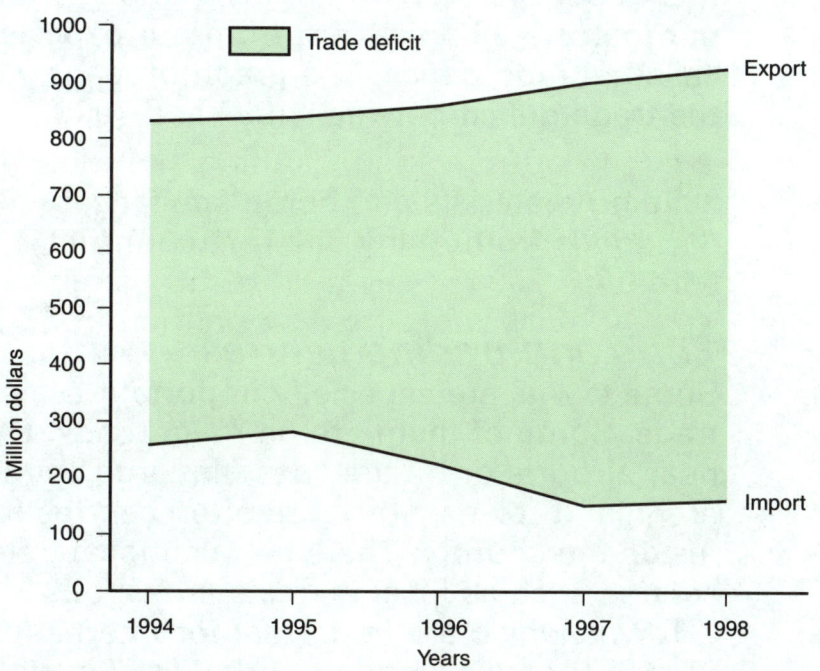

Balance of trade

Like many other Caribbean countries St Lucia spends more money on imports than it earns from exports. In 1994 total imports were worth EC$ 816.6 million; total exports were EC$ 254.7 million. We call the relationship between imports and exports the *balance of trade*.

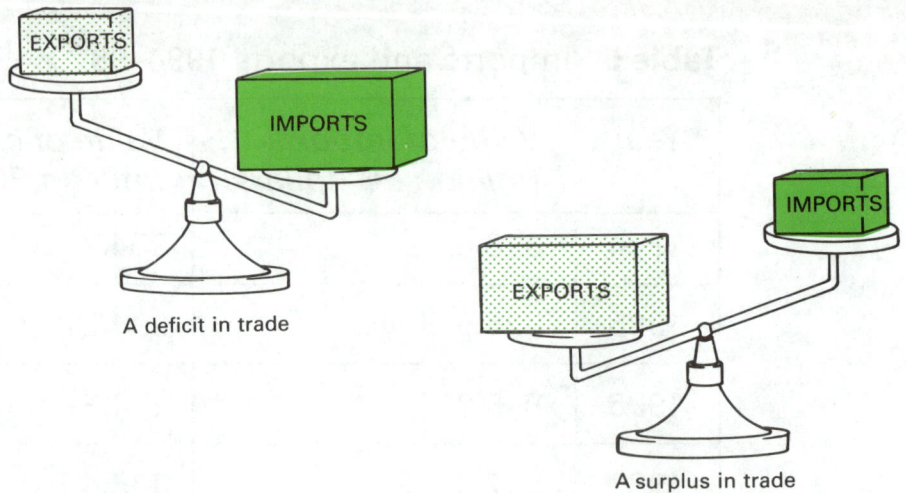

A deficit in trade

A surplus in trade

Look at the diagram. Why do you think we use the word 'balance' of trade when we talk about imports and exports?

It is important that we do not spend more money on our imports than we earn from our exports. This is called a trade *deficit*. The graph on page 71 shows the trade deficit between 1994 and 1998.

Why is it important that we do not spend too much more money on our imports than we earn from our exports?

Ports and trading centres

Some towns are especially important as centres for trade. Some of them are on main roads. Others are near airports or on the coast. In large countries there are inland towns which are often centres for trade inside the country. There are also local trading centres such as local markets and shops.

Towns which are important for international trade (that is for export and imports), are usually on the coast. These are called ports.

Why are trading centres for international trade usually on the coast?

Ports in our country

The ports of Castries and Vieux Fort are the two important seaports in our country.

Bananas travelling by road to port

Port Castries

Port Castries is one of the leading seaports in the Eastern Caribbean. The port first became important a long time ago when ships used steam to run their engines. These steam ships used to call at the Castries port to collect coal. This coal was used as fuel to provide the steam. Port Castries was rather like a present-day gas station. When steam ships were replaced with diesel vessels, Castries port had to take on other work. It became the main centre in St Lucia for import and export of goods. The photograph (above right) shows bananas loading at Castries.

By the middle of the 1960s it was realised that the existing port had to be expanded and modernised. The St Lucia Port Authority, and later the St Lucia Air and Seaports Authority, were formed to manage air and sea ports in St Lucia. Since then, many improvements have been made to the Castries Port.

A large quantity of the goods come in large containers. This makes the goods easier to handle and also reduces damage. In 1990, the Castries port had the capacity to store over 3000 containers and there was more than 1100 sq m (11 840 sq ft) of covered storage space for cargo.

73

Vieux Fort

All the bananas grown on the island are loaded at the seaport in Vieux Fort. From here they travel in ships to Europe. Land has been reclaimed from the sea in order to improve the port and make it a modern one. It is now able to accommodate container cargo. A pier over 185 metres (600 ft) long was built to accommodate roll-on/roll-off handling of cargo.

One of the reasons for developing Port Vieux Fort into a major port is to have it operating as a transhipment port.

What is a transhipment port?

Hewanorra Airport

Hewanorra Airport is St Lucia's main airport. It is situated in Vieux Fort.

Most of the visitors who come to our country come in through Hewanorra Airport. There are regular flights from the United States of America, England, Germany, Canada and the rest of the Caribbean area.

Since its construction the airport has undergone major improvements. The runway and taxiway have been upgraded, the parking aprons have been widened and a new passenger terminal built. This is needed because of the increasing number of travellers who use Hewanorra Airport. Better airport facilities will help in our country's efforts to develop further tourism and the industrial sectors of our economy.

Consumers

We call the person who makes or grows something a producer. We call the person who buys and uses the product a consumer. All of us are consumers because we all use things produced by others. Even the producer is a consumer also. Consumers use money to pay for what they buy. They need to use their money carefully.

Priscillia at Wood Green

Here is a short play about a girl named Priscillia. Priscillia and her mother have gone on holiday from St Lucia to London. The day after they arrive, they visit the Wood Green shopping centre in North London. Priscillia sees some apples on display at a grocer's store.

1 Read the play and notice what happens when Priscillia wants to buy the apples.
2 Act out the play in class.

PRISCILLIA:	(taking a $5.00 EC note from her bag) Wait, Mum, let me buy some of these nice apples.
MOTHER:	(not realising that it is EC currency), Who gave you the money? how much is it?
PRISCILLIA:	I took it from my cash pan just before we left St Lucia.
MOTHER:	(laughing) Oh no, my dear, you cannot buy things here with the money you have!
PRISCILLIA:	(looking puzzled) Why can't I?
MOTHER:	Well, you have EC dollars. This is the name of our money in St Lucia. Here in England, their money is different from ours. It is called Pound Sterling. Most people just say 'Pounds'.
PRISCILLIA:	But how will we be able to buy things, Mum?
MOTHER:	Cheer up, my dear. The day before we left home I went to the bank with some EC dollars and exchanged them for pounds. Here is a five-pound note. (She hands over the money).
PRISCILLIA:	Thanks, Mum, I'll buy some apples now.
MOTHER:	Before you do, let me explain. Just as one EC dollar is made up of 100 cents, the pound consists of 100 units. These units are called pence. In other words there are 100 in a pound.
PRISCILLIA:	So you check the pence in the pound just as you check the cents in our dollar?

MOTHER:	That is right! If the apples cost £1.80 – one pound and eighty pence – how much change should you receive from the five pound note?
PRISCILLIA:	Three pounds and twenty pence.
MOTHER:	That is correct. You can get your apples now.
PRISCILLIA:	So Mum, whenever someone travels to another country she must get the money which they use in that country?
MOTHER:	Yes, if that country does not use the same kind of money as ours.

Our currency

The money we have to buy goods with will only buy things in our own country. This is called our *currency*. Other countries have their own currency. In the story Priscillia had to use pounds when she went shopping.

Our currency is called the **Eastern Caribbean Currency**. Sometimes it is called simply EC Currency. Our currency consists of dollar notes and coins representing different amounts of cents. There are some dollar coins also. One EC dollar is worth one hundred cents. Look at some dollar notes.

Most of the other countries of the Eastern Caribbean share the EC dollar. If we were to travel to any of these countries there will be no need for us to find another currency.

 ▪ ▪ Make a list of the countries which share the EC currency with our country. Find them on a map of the Caribbean in your atlas. Which countries in the Eastern Caribbean do *not* share our EC currency?

The law

Our government makes laws to make sure that the people who trade do not cheat anyone. If you go to a shop you will notice that there is a scale which is used to weigh many of the goods such as sugar, flour and chicken. The butchers and fishermen also use a scale. Most of the goods which are sold in bags or packages in the supermarkets have been weighed to ensure that the correct amounts are put into the packages. If shopkeepers, butchers and fishermen tamper with their scales to cheat their customers, they may be acting against the law.

Government tries to protect consumers by having

price control on some types of goods. This means that the Ministry of Trade tells the merchants the highest price that can be asked for an item or a certain amount of it. Some officers of the Ministry of Trade can take shopkeepers, fishermen or butchers to court if they sell their goods above what is stated by government. (Not all goods are under price control.)

Another very important law prevents shopkeepers and merchants from selling poor goods to people. People who sell meat and fish, for example, must make sure that these do not contain germs which can cause the people who buy them to become ill. Sometimes, officers of the Ministry of Health go into business places and collect items such as rusty tins and spoiled meats for dumping. Health officers also visit restaurants to make certain that the food prepared in their eating houses is prepared and served under clean conditions.

Look at the diagram on page 77. What do we mean by the 'legal umbrella'?

There are also laws regarding the import and export of goods. When people import and export goods they must pay duties according to the type and amount of goods. The Customs Department tries to ensure that all imports and exports are done according to government regulations. People can be charged large sums of money for breaking customs regulations. The government, through the Customs Department, can even place a ban on certain types of goods from coming into the country.

A TRADING DIARY
Keep a trading diary for a week of everything your family buys. Ask your parents and your brothers and sisters to tell you what they have bought so that you can note it down. At the end of the week, note where the things come from. How far did they travel to get to you?

WHICH IS TRUE?

Copy out the statements below. Beside each statement write True or False.

Many of our tourists come from North America.

Very few people from other Caribbean islands visit St Lucia.

Desruisseaux is one of our main ports.

Port Castries is a container port.

Every one of us is a consumer.

We can use Eastern Caribbean dollars anywhere in the world.

A trading deficit means that we have exported more goods than we have imported.

All foreign currency must be kept safely at home.

Our main exports are bananas and coconut oil.

If you buy a pen that does not work you should take it back to the shop and complain politely.

Choose the best answer to each of the following questions. Write the question and the answer in your notebook. Some questions refer to the diagram below.

Caribbean tourist arrivals 1990

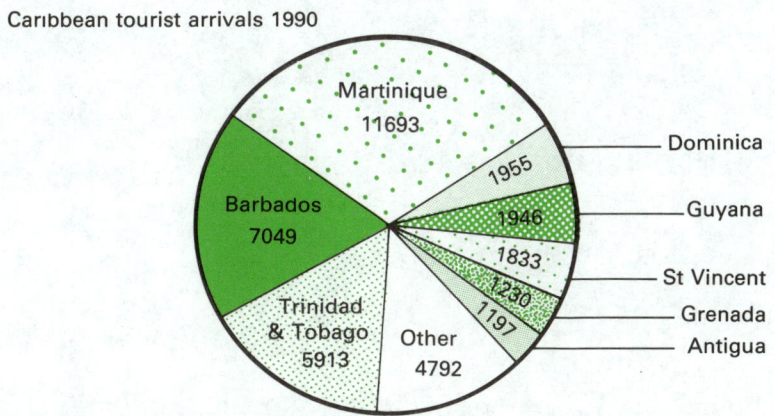

Source: St Lucia Tourist Board, Tourism Statistical Analysis 1990

1 Tourists come to our country for all of these except
  A sightseeing   **B** Carnival
  C work   **D** enjoying the climate.

2 The cruise-ship terminal of St Lucia is at
  A Castries   **B** Vieux Fort
  C Point Seraphine   **D** Soufriere.

3 The slice of the pie chart marked **other** includes
  A non-Caribbean countries   **B** Jamaica
  C United States   **D** UK.

4 Most Caribbean tourists in 1990 came from
  A Martinique   **B** Barbados
  C Antigua   **D** Jamaica.

TOPIC

5

Our government

When people come together to form a group there is often someone who directs the activities of the group. These people are called leaders. There are leaders in your family. They are your parents. The leaders at your school are the principal and teachers. They may also be called the staff. There are many other leaders in the community.

Name some leaders in your community.
List some of the things which these leaders do.

We also have national leaders. We call the group of persons who lead our nation **our government**. Our government is very important because these leaders make laws and provide services for the good of the whole country.

Election time

In *Caribbean Social Studies 3*, we learned about local government. We had an election in class. We chose a candidate and voted by raising hands.

Have another election. Let different pupils stand for election this time. Instead of raising your hands, vote by **SECRET BALLOT**. This means that you write on a piece of paper the name of the candidate you vote for. The teacher will count the votes and tell you who had the largest number. Do you think secret ballot is a better way of voting than raising hands. Why?

Our national government

The principal and the teachers group together to run the school. There is a group of people who are responsible for running the whole country. This group of people is called the government. Just as the group of people who run the school has a leader — the principal — the group of people who form the government also has a leader. In our country the leader of the government is called the **prime minister**. The Head of State is the Governor.

We live in a *democratic* country. This means that the people of our country have the right to choose the people whom they want to lead the country. People who agree about how the country should be run, form groups called **political parties**. They then begin to hold meetings explaining to people what they intend to do for them and for the country, if they are chosen to form the government.

On **election day** the people who are old enough to vote go to the **polling stations** and vote for the person of their choice. They vote behind a screen so

The Governor's Residence on the Morne

that no one can see whom they vote for. At the end of the day all the votes in all parts of the country are counted. The party which wins the most seats forms the government. The others form the **opposition**. The leader of the winning group becomes the prime minister and the leader of the group with the next largest number is called the **leader of the opposition**.

How old must someone in our country be before he or she is allowed to vote?

When an election is over all the people who are elected become members of the House of Assembly. When we address these people we use the word 'honourable' before their name. In our country not all the members of government are elected. Some people are appointed or nominated to help in making good laws for the country. These members form a special group called the **Senate**. Members of the House of Assembly and the Senate are together called members of PARLIAMENT.

Before a law is made in our country it is discussed by the members of the House of Assembly, and after that by the members of the Senate. If both the House of Assembly and the Senate agree with the bill it becomes a law.

1 Answer these questions in your exercise book.
   a) Name the political parties in our country.
   b) Who is the leader of each political party?
   c) Which of the leaders is the Prime Minister?
   d) Who is the leader of the opposition?
2 In your exercise book write a heading: **Members of Government in Our Country**. Under this heading, draw two columns and head them — **Members who are elected** and **Members who are appointed or nominated**. Write under each column the names of the members of the government who fit each column.
   Your teacher will help you.

The role of the state

All citizens of our country have certain rights. On the day of our independence we adopted a constitution which assured us of certain basic rights and freedoms called **Fundamental Rights and Freedoms**. Three of these basic rights are those relating to protection of life and property, freedom of expression and freedom of belief or freedom of conscience.

It is the duty of our government leaders to ensure that our fundamental rights are protected. It is their duty also to help us meet certain basic needs and provide us with certain services. Special people are employed by the government to help it provide these services. These people are called **public servants**.

Here are some of the most important services which our government must provide.

1 Education
One of these important services is education. In order for the country to develop, its people must be educated. This is why different types of schools have to be built to educate the people. The public servants who help to achieve this are the teachers.

Name the schools in your community or district.

2 Health care
The people of the nation must also be kept healthy. The government also provides medical care for the people. The nurses and doctors who work in the health centres and hospitals help to provide this service.

Look back at the study of Nurse Leslie's work at Mon Repos Health Centre on page 61. How does her work help to keep people healthy?

3 Transport and communication

As the country develops, people need to move from place to place. Some travel abroad on business or on holiday. Some travel to shop and sell their produce. Others go to and from work, and many children travel to school. In order to make such travel possible, government has to build and maintain roads and airports.

People also need to communicate with others both near and far. It is also the task of the government to make sure that people are able to communicate easily. This is why we have the postal, telephone, telegram, telex, facsimile and e-mail services.

4 Protection

People must be protected from others who may want to be unfair to them or to cause them injury. In other words, we can say that people's rights must be respected. To keep the peace, laws must be made to guide the way people behave.

Explain why it is good that laws are made to protect people.

When the government makes laws, the police and the courts must see that these laws are obeyed. If in the opinion of the police someone has committed an **offence** (broken the law), this person is **charged** and taken to court. During the court session, the magistrate decides whether the person is guilty of the offence or not. If he or she is guilty, the magistrate decides what punishment should be given.

Telecommunications Building

List some other services which the government provides for the people of our country. Which of these does the photograph above show?

Revenue

The State has to have money in order to provide these services. Some of this money comes from the people of our country in the form of taxes, duties and licences. It is called *revenue*.

One of the most common forms of tax paid to the government is **income tax**. This is an amount of money which is deducted from people's wages and salaries (their 'income') and paid to the government. In our country, income tax is paid by the system called **Pay As You Earn** (PAYE). This means that, generally, the more money you earn the more income tax you pay, and the less you earn the less you pay. Some people whose wages or salaries are small do not pay any tax at all. Of course, it isn't always that simple!

We learned in Topic 4 that people pay duties when they import and export goods. When goods are manufactured in the country, tax is paid to the government on each of the items which are sold. This is called **consumption tax**. People who own vehicles, shops, restaurants pay yearly licences to the government.

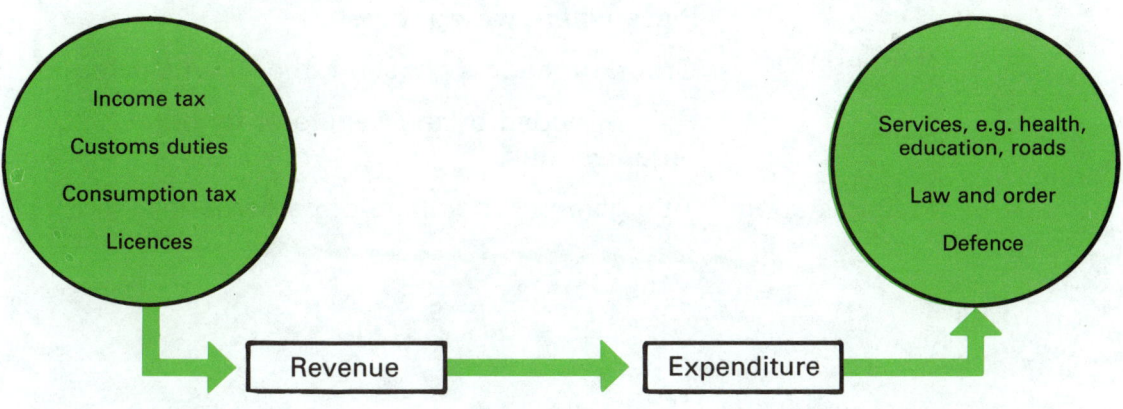

Income tax
Customs duties
Consumption tax
Licences

Services, e.g. health, education, roads
Law and order
Defence

Revenue → Expenditure

■ ■ **1** Make a list of other licences which people pay to the government.
2 Find out what local revenue is used for. What services are provided by your local council? In what ways could they be improved?

MATCHING

Copy these columns in your exercise book and draw a line from each of the words on the left to the statement on the right which matches it.

Revenue	Money which people pay to the government from their salaries or wages.
Secret ballot	People who wish to be elected as leaders.
Candidates	A group of leaders who look after a country.
Government	Money collected by the government in order to pay for services.
Prime Minister	Democratic way in which people choose national leaders.
Income tax	Leader of the members of parliament who form the government.
Elections	Method of voting which prevents other people from knowing for whom you voted.
Services	Place where we go to vote.
Honourable	Group of leaders chosen rather than elected.
Senate	Help provided by the Senate or by other organisations.
Polling station	Title given to members of parliament.

Our independent nation

National symbols

Our flag

Our country, St Lucia, is an independent nation. We have a flag which is flown from public buildings, and on other buildings on special occasions.

Our national flag was designed by Mr Dunstan St Omer. It consists of a blue background on which three triangles with a common base are placed. The triangle at the bottom is of a golden colour. The black is placed over the gold and the white triangle comes over the black one. You can see a colour picture of our flag on the back cover of this book.

The blue in our flag represents our blue sky and the blue oceans which surround us. The golden triangle represents the sunshine. The black and white ones represent the black and white cultures which help to shape the culture of our country. They also indicate that both black and white people live and work in harmony with each other. The triangle shape was also chosen to represent the shape of the Pitons.

Our coat of arms

The Coat of Arms is another of our national symbols.

On the back cover of this book there is a colour picture of the Coat of Arms. On page 90 there is a diagram showing the different features of it. Look carefully at these pictures as you read the following explanation of the features of the Coat of Arms.

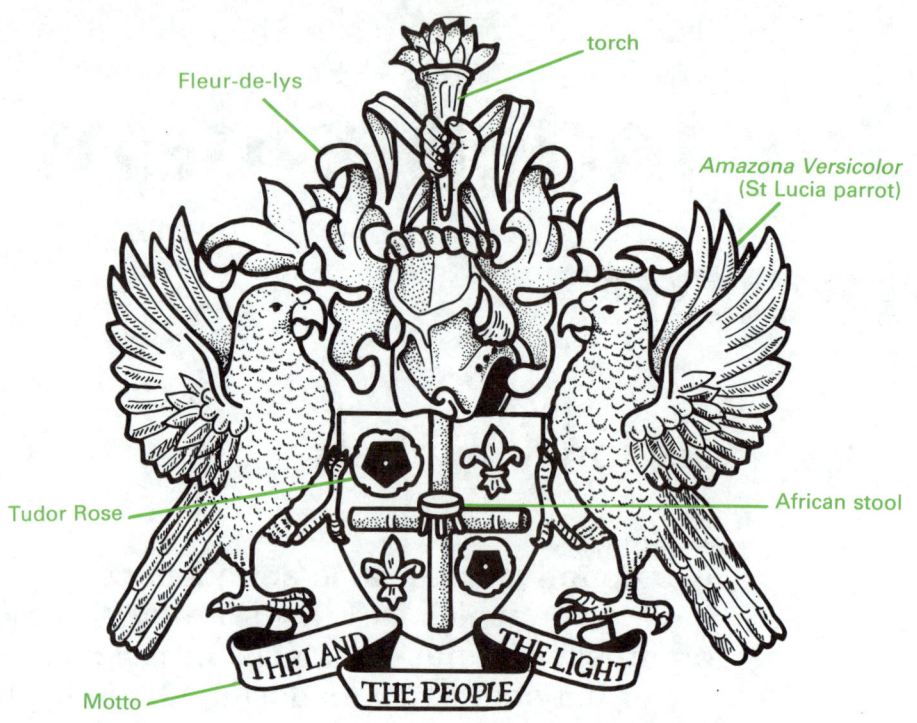

The Coat of Arms consists of two parrots. These are the *Amazona Versicolor*, our national bird. The torch at the top represents a beacon to light our path throughout the development of our nation. The flowers on the Coat of Arms are the Tudor Rose and the Fleur-de-lys. They serve to remind us of England and France, the two countries which ruled our nation. The African stool reminds us of our African ancestry.

OUR MOTTO:
Beneath the Coat of Arms is a *motto*. Our country's motto is 'the Land, the People, the Light': **'the Land'** indicates that we need to cultivate (grow crops in) and develop our land. **'The People'** means that the people must be educated so that they can develop themselves and their country. **'The Light'** signifies a lighted path to guide us along.

Our national anthem
We have a national song which we sing on special occasions. Some of these special occasions are National Day, Remembrance Day and Independence

Day parade. We also sing the national anthem during school assemblies. The national anthem is played just before the Prime Minister addresses the nation on radio or on television. In some countries radio and television stations play the national anthem just before they begin broadcasting in the morning and when they end at night.

Do any of the radio or television stations do this in our country?

Here are the words of our national anthem.

The words were written by Rev. Father Charles Jesse and the music was written by Leton Thomas.

Sons and Daughters of St Lucia,
Love the land that gave us birth
Land of beaches, hills and valleys,
Fairest isle of all the earth
Wheresoever you may roam, love,
Oh love our island home.

Gone the times when nations battled
For this 'Helen of the West'!
Gone the days when strife and discord
Dimmed her children's toil and rest
Dawns at last a brighter day
Stretches out a glad new way.

May the good Lord bless our island
Guard her sons from woe and harm!
May our people live united,
Strong in soul, and strong in arm,
Justice, Truth and Charity
Our ideal forever be!

1 Learn the words of our national song so that you can sing them at the next celebration.
2 Write in one or two sentences the main ideas of the song.

Other symbols

After independence our country selected other national symbols.

The calabash

The calabash is our national tree. Trees can grow to heights of over fifteen feet. The flowers are yellowish and the calabash fruit can be over two feet in circumference.

Although the calabash was much more useful to people in the past it is still quite useful to many. Long ago, before many people had metal and plastic baskets and pails, the calabash was used for collecting water from the rivers and springs. Many farmers still use calabash dishes for eating in their gardens. Members of the Rastafarian community use the calabash as one of their main utensils.

Calabashes of various sizes are also used for making ornaments.

The bamboo

Like the calabash, the bamboo has been chosen as a national plant. Bamboo poles of various sizes have been used by the people of our country throughout our history.

Long ago, before there were roads in rural communities people had to carry their sick in hammocks. Dry bamboo poles were used in making these hammocks. Bamboo has been used throughout our history to make various kinds of fish pots. Some of these pots are placed in rivers but they are more often placed in the sea. People also use bamboo to make ornaments and even furniture.

How is bamboo used in the Christmas season?

Bamboo plants grow in clumps and they produce very many fibrous roots. These help to hold the soil together and in doing so prevent soil erosion.

The bamboo has therefore been a very useful plant throughout our country's history.

Our national flowers

Our country's national flowers are the **Rose** and the **Marguerite**. They were selected in 1985. You can see pictures of these flowers on page 41.

The rose is more common as it can be seen all over the island. It is popular because of its sweet perfumed smell. It is regarded as a symbol of beauty.

The marguerite is a small round flower. It is purple or white in colour. Unlike the rose, the marguerite does not have a perfumed smell but it looks beautiful when growing in small clumps or, when mixed with other flowers in preparing a bouquet.

What is a **bouquet**?

Our two flower festivals have taken their names from the rose and marguerite flowers.

Our national bird

The St Lucian parrot is officially called the *Amazona Versicolor*. It is commonly called 'Jacquot'. There are several species of parrots in the Caribbean but the *Amazona Versicolor* is native to St Lucia. Many people think 'Jacquot' is the most beautiful bird on the island.

During the 1980s the parrot population had become small mainly because people hunted them or cut down the trees which the birds fed and nested in. Now our national bird, like all other birds in the forest, is protected by law. Anyone found hunting the parrot can be fined up to $5000.

People's attitude towards our national bird has changed. Now most people see the parrot as 'a symbol of beauty' rather than a bird to be shot and eaten.

Our national dress

Our national dress is worn today during certain types of cultural activities and on special occasions such as during National and Independence Day Celebration.

The National dress is based on the type of dress which was commonly worn by ladies long ago. This dress was usually called the **Jupe** and **Wob Douillette**: this consists of a large petticoat and skirt.

The head was tied with a scarf, which was called a **Madwas**. The madwas was tied with peaks at the top. A married woman had one peak, while an unmarried lady had three. It is said that those with two peaks indicated that they were engaged.

Make a wall display with the title 'National Symbols'. Find or draw pictures of the national flag, the coat of arms, the *Amazona Versicolor*, the calabash tree, our national flowers and our national dress. Write out the words of the national anthem to put on your wall display. Learn the words of the national anthem if you do not already know them. Sing it proudly in school assembly.

National monuments

In our country we have some special places which remind us of important people and events in our country.

Pigeon Peninsula

Just north of the village of Gros Islet is Pigeon Peninsula. This area was a small island until it was joined to the mainland by a causeway (see photograph above).

Historians believe that Pigeon Island was first inhabited by Caribs. Later it become a hideout for a pirate called Francois Le Clerk. He was nicknamed 'Jambe de Bois' because he had a wooden leg. There was a cave on the northern side of the islet, but the roof has since caved in. Le Clerk used this cave to hide treasures captured from passing ships.

In 1979 Pigeon Peninsula was officially opened as a National Park. Soon a National museum will be established in the area. Visitors to the park can see the remains of military buildings which were constructed by British soldiers. Fort Rodney, at the top of the southern peak is a popular visiting spot.

The Morne

Morne Fortune was the scene of many battles between the English and the French, as they fought to capture St Lucia from each other. During this time the Morne was made the military headquarters of these nations.

The remains of some of the military buildings can still be seen. The larger ones have been *renovated* and now serve as the major buildings of the Sir Arthur Lewis Community College. Military buildings at Vigie are also being made useful like this.

At the top of the Morne a few yards to the east of the present Division of Arts, Science, and General Studies main building is the Inniskilling Memorial. This monument marks the capture of the Morne by the British from a group of French revolutionary forces on 24 May 1796.

In the south-western part of the Morne are the military cemeteries where governors, military persons and members of the families of both the English and the French are buried.

Much more recently, one of our country's governors, Sir Ira Simmons, was buried in the military cemetery on the Morne. The Morne is the burial site of one of our country's greatest sons, Sir Arthur Lewis, after whom the College was named. He is buried on the grounds of the College close to the Division of Arts, Science and General Studies.

Castries Roman Catholic Cathedral, Derek Walcott Square

Derek Walcott Square

This recreational area near the Castries Catholic Cathedral was named 'Columbus Square' in 1893. On 23 January 1993 it was re-named Derek Walcott Square, after the great St Lucian poet. You will learn more about Derek Walcott on page 99.

In the centre of the square is a Cenotaph. This is a monument dedicated to the St Lucians who died during the world wars. Remembrance ceremonies are held in November of each year to mark the occasion.

During National Day and Independence Celebrations many activities such as the Festival of Lights, parades and other cultural performances are held at the Square. Derek Walcott Square is still used as a place for relaxation especially in the evenings when the city has become much quieter.

Two great men from St Lucia

Several men and women have helped our country to develop. However two of these have been recognised all over the world for their work. They have been awarded **Nobel Prizes**. They are Sir Arthur Lewis and Derek Walcott.

Sir William Arthur Lewis

Sir William Arthur Lewis was born in St Lucia on 23 January, 1915. After completing his secondary education he worked for a short time as a civil servant in St Lucia. He then went to England to study Economics.

Sir Arthur was an outstanding scholar. He started teaching at the university level at the age of twenty-three. He taught in England and the United States. He also wrote many articles and books on Economics.

Sir Arthur Lewis advised many governments. These included Ghana, Nigeria, Trinidad & Tobago, and Barbados. He served as Vice Chancellor of The University of the West Indies, and was the first President of The Caribbean Development Bank. He was awarded the Nobel Prize for his outstanding work in Economics, in 1979.

Sir Arthur died in June 1991. He is buried on the grounds of the College at the Morne which carries his name, The Sir Arthur Lewis Community College.

Derek Walcott

Derek Walcott is one of the world's greatest poets. He was born in St Lucia on 23 January, 1930. Derek started writing poetry when he was about 16. He was also interested in writing plays. His first major play was called "Henri Christophe", based on the Haitian Revolution during the period of slavery.

After graduating from secondary school, Derek went to study in Jamaica. During his period of study in Jamaica his talents as a poet continued to blossom. He taught in St Lucia and Grenada after returning from university.

Derek then settled in Trinidad where he founded a Theatre Group. He won many awards for his poems and plays.

In 1990 Derek Walcott was among the first group of Caribbean Citizens to receive the Caribbean Community's Outstanding Citizens Award.

The greatest moment of Derek Walcott's career so far came on 8 October, 1992, when he was awarded the Nobel Prize for Literature.

We are proud of our great sons. No other country of our size has produced two Nobel Laureates!

Ask your teacher to arrange a visit to some national monuments. Write notes for a project book called **Our National Monuments**.

Important events in our country

At the beginning of the chapter we read that our country is independent. This means that we must take care of all our own affairs. The governments of England or France can no longer take decisions for us.

Before we became independent many important events took place in our country which we should remember.

1 Look at the **time line** on page 102. A time line shows important events with the dates at which they happened. Read on for more details of the events which occurred on each of these dates. Write a sentence about what happened on the following dates:

1605	1659	1664	1765	1780
1796–7	1834	1871	1887	1889
1938	1948	1958	1979	

2 Make a note of other dates mentioned in this topic as you read about them. Note down what happened at this date.

3 Play the History Game on page 106.

Dates and events

1605 A British ship called the *Olive Branch* (or *Oliph Blossom*), while on its way to South America, was forced to land on the south-eastern coast of St Lucia near Vieux Fort. At first the men got along well with the Caribs but trouble started after a few weeks. In the end only 19 of them managed to escape to Venezuela in a large canoe.

1659 The British and the French began their disputes over St Lucia.

1664 An army of 1000 Englishmen who had settled on the island of Barbados attacked St Lucia with the help of a group of Caribs. The British claimed that they had bought the island from the Caribs the previous year.

1765 The sugar industry was established in St Lucia.

1780 A devastating hurricane struck St Lucia during the night of 10-11 October. Most of the crops and buildings on the island were destroyed. Even the churches on the island were blown down.

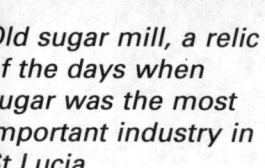

Old sugar mill, a relic of the days when sugar was the most important industry in St Lucia

1794/7 Trouble raged in St Lucia between the French and the British. The French Republicans who had taken part in the French Revolution sent their agents to the Caribbean. They took over St Lucia and freed slaves. In 1796 the British under General Moors recaptured the island. Many of the Republicans and slaves went into the hills and carried out *guerrilla warfare* against the British, killing and burning. This went on until 1797 when they finally surrendered. These people were called **Brigands**. When the British took over, slavery was re-established.

1834 On 1 August 1834 all slaves in St Lucia became free. They became what was known as **apprenticed labourers**.

1838 The apprenticed labourers became fully free. This is also called **Emancipation of the Slaves**. The first Mico schools were established in St Lucia.

1887/9 Victoria Hospital was opened in 1887. It was named after Queen Victoria who celebrated her golden jubilee (being Queen for fifty years) in that year. In 1889 the first secondary school on the island, St Mary's College, was established.

1600

1700

1800

1900

1605

The *Olive Branch* forced to land near Vieux Fort

1659

British and French dispute over St Lucia begins

1664

St Lucia attacked by British with Carib help

1765

Sugar industry established

1780

Hurricane strikes St Lucia

1794

French Republicans take over St Lucia and free slaves

1796

British recapture St Lucia

1797

Brigands surrender, slavery returns

1834

Slaves freed

1887

Victoria Hospital opened

1927

Fire destroys government offices in Castries

1938

Heavy rains cause landslide in Ravine Poisson, killing many

1941

American bases established in Gros Islet

1958

St Lucia becomes part of West Indies Federation

1967

Castries granted status of city

1979

St Lucia gains full independence

1927 A serious fire destroyed many houses and government offices in the town of Castries.

1938 Very heavy rains caused landslides in Ravine Poisson area. Almost one hundred lives were lost.

1941 American soldiers started establishing bases in St Lucia, firstly in Gros Islet and later in Vieux Fort.

1948 On the night of 19–20 June of 1948, about 80% of Castries was destroyed again by fire. Over 2000 people were made homeless as a result of the fire.

1958 St Lucia became part of the West Indies Federation which linked many of the Caribbean islands which Britain ruled. However, the Federation ended in 1962.

1967 Castries was also granted the status of city and Joseph Desir became the Major of Castries.

1979 On 22 February 1979 our country became fully independent from Britain.

Steps towards independence

The people of St Lucia wanted to have more say in their government. They wanted to have *self-government*. In 1951 *adult suffrage* was introduced. This meant that every adult had the right to vote at elections. On 1 January 1960 there was a change in the *constitution*. This allowed St Lucia to have a Chief Minister as head of the government. After the general elections of 1961 St Lucia had its first Chief Minister, George Charles.

On 1 March 1967 St Lucia became an **associated state**. This was another step on the road to independence. Sir Frederick Clarke became our country's first Governor.

On 22 February 1979 full independence was achieved. The Premier, John Compton, became our country's first Prime Minister. You can see him in the picture on page 106.

HISTORY GAME

On page 105 there is a picture of a game board. Copy the board on to a large piece of card, about 60 cm by 40 cm. Draw the map of St Lucia in the middle. Make 12 game cards exactly the same size as the spaces marked around the outside of the game board. Copy the text for each card from the list below. Place the pile of cards upside down in the middle of the board.

Play the game like this. Each player takes a card from the pile of cards in the middle of the board. The player must decide where the card should go on the board, choosing the correct date. If he or she chooses the correct space, one point is scored. If not, the next player may place the card. If this player puts the card in the correct place, two points are scored for that player. When all the cards have been used up, the player with the most points is the winner.

If players cannot agree as to the correct place for a card, check on pages 101-103 of this book.

The *Olive Branch* lands in St Lucia

Hurricane strikes St Lucia and destroys most buildings

French Republican agents come to St Lucia and free slaves

Emancipation of the Slaves

Ravine Poisson landslide

Castries fire makes 2000 people homeless

West Indies Federation is set up

St Lucia becomes a fully independent country

Victoria Hospital is opened and named after Queen of England

Adult suffrage is achieved in St Lucia

British and Caribs attack St Lucia

Sugar industry established in St Lucia

1780	1765	1664	1605
1794			1979
1838	Event Cards		1958
1887	1938	1948	1951

Sir John Compton, first Prime Minister of St Lucia (centre) with leaders from other Caribbean countries, at a conference in Barbados in 1988

 WRITING SENTENCES

Write a few sentences on **five** of the following:

a) *Amazona Versicolor*;
b) our national flag;
c) the Coat of Arms;
d) our national flowers;
e) calabash and bamboo;
f) steps to independence;
g) Pigeon Peninsula and the Morne;
h) Derek Walcott Square.

Choose one of our national heroes. Write a few sentences about his life and work, and say why you admire him.

Glossary

adult suffrage   the vote for every adult

agricultural   to do with farming (agriculture)

archaeologist   someone who finds out about the past by digging up things left behind by earlier people.

artefacts   things which have been made by people

balance of trade   relationship between the value of imports and the value of exports

bay   sheltered area of sea almost enclosed by land

beverage   something to drink, alcoholic or non-alcoholic

capital   place from which a country is governed

city   very large town

coastal strip   land close to the sea

commercial   to do with business or making money

constitution   a set of rules by which we are governed

creole   mixed language or culture, often developed in a colony

cruise-ship passengers   visitors who come to our country in cruise ships

culture   customs and ideas which make a people special

currency   system of notes and coins used as money

data   information recorded for use

deficit   a situation where more money is spent than is earned

define   say exactly what a word means

democratic   ruled by an elected government

disaster   sudden terrible event which leaves damage and distress behind it

dramatise   make something come to life by acting

employment   work for which somebody else pays you

environment   our surroundings, especially its natural features

erode   wear away

extinct   does not erupt any more

facilities   things which make life or work easier, e.g. schools, churches, cinemas (also called **amenities**)

fertile   full of nutrients for growing crops

guerrilla warfare   small-scale war fought by small groups of soldiers

human resources   work of human beings

indigenous   having lived in an area for many thousands of years

industrial   to do with industry

irrigate   provide water for crops when there is not enough rainfall

location   the exact position where a thing or a person or a place is found

manufacturing industry   making things in a factory

market   place or people to which goods are sold

meteorologist   a weather expert

mountain range   group of mountains

motto   special phrase which is chosen to represent a country, family or organisation, e.g. on a coat of arms

non-renewable   not able to replace itself naturally

origin   beginning, usually far in the past

peninsula   piece of land surrounded on three sides by water

physical features   natural features in our landscape

pollute   spoil by adding dirty or dangerous things

raw materials   material suitable for manufacture

reclaim   restore land which is covered by water so that it can be used

renewable   able to replace itself naturally

renovate   make as good as new

resources   things around us which we can use

revenue   money paid to the State so that services can be provided

rural   of the country rather than the town

self-government   rule by the local people, not by another country

soil erosion   wearing away of the soil

squatting   living in a place without any legal right to do so

subsistence   producing food only for our own family

urban   of the town rather than the country